Ellen DeGeneres
HOME

GRAND CENTRAL

Life & Style

NEW YORK • BOSTON

Grand Central Life & Style
Hachette Book Group
1290 Avenue of the Americas
New York, NY 10104
GrandCentralLifeandStyle.com
Printed in the United States of America

WOR

First Edition: October 2015

10 9 8 7 6 5 4 3 2 1

Grand Central Life & Style is an imprint of Grand Central Publishing.

The Grand Central Life & Style name and logo are trademarks of Hachette Book Group, Inc.

The Hachette Speakers Bureau provides a wide range of authors for speaking events. To find out more, go to www.HachetteSpeakersBureau.com or call (866) 376-6591.

The publisher is not responsible for websites (or their content) that are not owned by the publisher.

Library of Congress Control Number: 2015940081

ISBNs: 978-1-4555-3356-5 (hardcover), 978-1-4555-3785-3 (special edition)

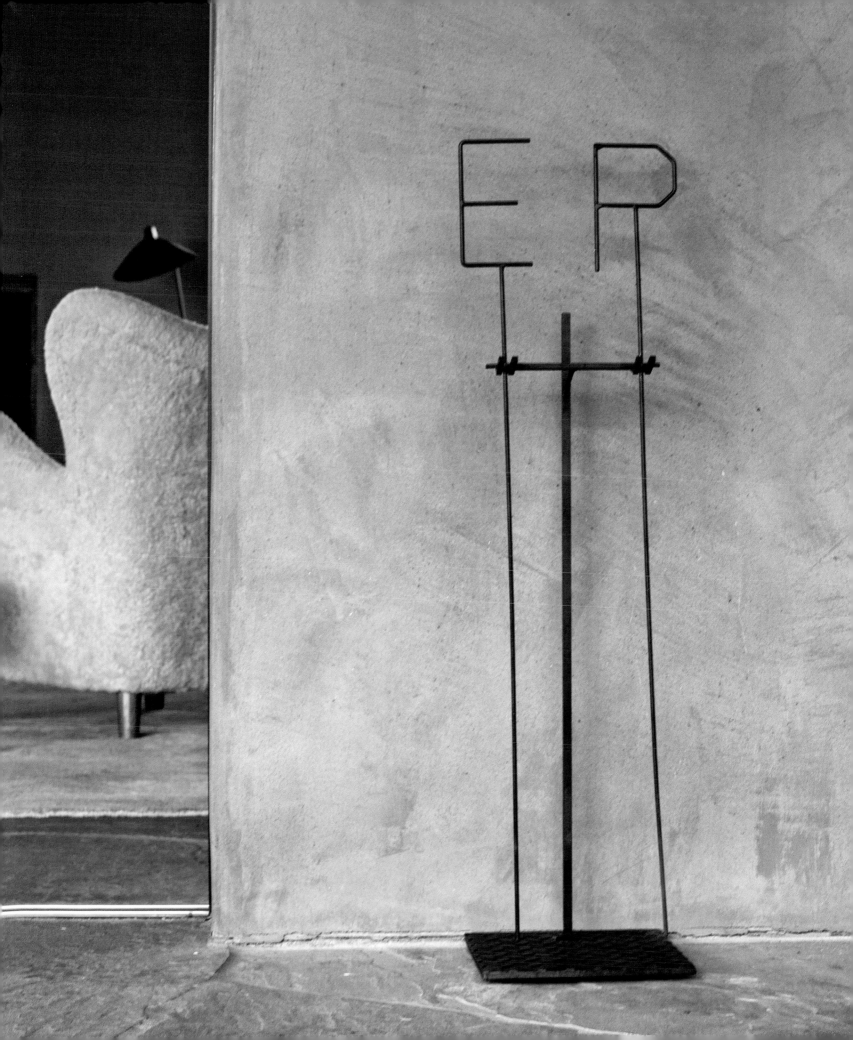

TABLE OF CONTENTS

INTRODUCTION

Hi, everyone! And welcome home. Welcome to *Home*. Welcome to my homes. Welcome. This book is all about—you're never gonna believe this—the home! It's about my current home, my former homes, what makes a home a home, and what you can do to make your home homier. The word "home" will appear in this book nine million times.

How do I know so much about this, you ask? Don't I usually write humorous books chock-full of observational anecdotes and sharp wit? Well, first of all, thank you for being so inquisitive and also complimentary. I wasn't expecting that. And the answer is this: I have had a passion for interior design for as long as I can remember. In fact, interior design is what I would do if I wasn't a comedian and talk show host. And when you really think about it, they're not that different. As a talk show host, I sit and talk with beautiful people all day. Some are young, some are a little older. They all have fun quirks that make them interesting and unique. They have a story to tell. They have outstanding bone structure, and yet what really matters is what's on the inside. It's the same with houses. Some are young, some are older. They all have quirks that make them interesting and unique. They have a story to tell and great bones, but what really matters is what's on the inside. And after you've spent a little bit of time with each one and learned what you can, it's time to bring out the next house. I mean, guest. I mean, both.

Yes, it's true. I move a lot. It's well documented. A lot of people don't understand it. Most folks grow up in one home and spend most of their adult life in another home, and to them that's normal. But for me and the conch shell crab, it's not normal. Normal to us is finding a shell that suits us for a while until we outgrow that shell and then find another shell to crawl into. But unlike the crab that chooses the same type of shell, each one bigger than the last, my taste in styles and sizes of homes is varied. I've gone from traditional to midcentury to contemporary to Italianate. I have downsized as often as I've upsized.

As corny as it sounds, to me, home is where the heart is. (Note to self: That's a great phrase. Look into trademarking.) So moving houses is just another way in which I get to experience life. I mean, I get that moving from house to house isn't appealing to everyone. After all, it's right up there in stressors with death and losing a job. In my case, I could add hosting the Oscars to that list, and moving houses two days after hosting the Oscars. But the truth is, moving has always been fun for me, not stressful. To understand why, you must first understand where my desire to constantly move comes from . . . and it's not just from writing an essay on conch shell crabs in the sixth grade.

My family moved a lot. Not out of state, just to different areas of the city of New Orleans, where I was born. And by living in different houses, I discovered that each one came with a different personality—different molding, different ceiling heights, different surfaces and floors. But we never owned any of these houses, only rented. So in addition to moving from rental to rental, we spent most Sundays as a family going to open houses. I not only loved seeing all the different types of architecture, from typical New Orleans bungalows to Spanish, ranch style, and traditional, but it was interesting to see how different people lived, the furniture they used, the way they decorated, what kind of food they had in the fridge, what kinds of medicine they were taking.

Although I wouldn't realize it until later, those Sundays spent at open houses were the beginning of my passion for design and owning houses. The houses I saw as a kid were probably about $60,000 to $80,000 (it was the '60s in New Orleans) and we couldn't afford them. I didn't know that at the time; I imagined each one of them might be our first home, especially if we went back to look at it a few times. But we never even made an offer. And that is why as soon as I was even close to being able to afford a house, I bought one.

My first house was $250,000, and at thirty years old, I was a homeowner. Once I was in the market it was easy to parlay that first house into another, better house (I discovered as an added bonus, real estate is a good investment), and as my career and my bank account kept growing, I found that all I wanted to do was find a new and better design project. My financial success in my career enabled my passion for design to grow as I learned about furniture and architecture with each new home.

So that's my story. I love houses and I love design. This book is a collection of houses I've lived in (or at least the ones I've photographed), stores where I love to shop for special pieces, and the houses of friends who inspire and educate me. You'll see themes running through each house, like a love of nature and a seamless feeling of indoor and outdoor spaces. You'll also see that there are some very simple, effortless things you can do to make little improvements to your own homes. Things like putting some lemons in a bowl. They provide instant cheer and a wonderful scent. I should point out that effortless doesn't mean lazy. You can't leave the lemons there until they start to mold and stink up the joint and be like "No, it's fine, Ellen said I should put lemons there last October." But for a while, they'll be a great addition to any room.

So I hope you enjoy this book du design (doesn't that sound French and fancy?! It's neither!) and I hope you learn a little something. I mean, you've already learned about the conch shell crab, and that was just the beginning.

ELLEN'S HOMES

Every weekend, Portia and I look at real estate listings. Actually, that's a lie. We look every day. It's our version of the comics. It's funny, though, because my favorite way to actually shop for homes is at dinner parties. This has happened a few times. We first saw this house when we were invited over to watch *American Idol,* and before we had seen three contestants sing, we were negotiating price/square footage with our host. So, what I'm saying is, don't invite us over unless you're ready to move out.

The main home was originally built by Buff & Hensman for actor Laurence Harvey in 1963, and it is has great bones (its footprint was expanded right before we bought it, which gave it a lot more square footage). And we could have (probably should have) stopped there. But we decided to make it even better by buying the two surrounding properties when they became available. It was very exciting to be able to buy those other homes. And it seemed like a good idea at the time, as it gave us total privacy, and what was pretty much a compound. It was a really beautiful property and we loved it there. In fact, we got married there.

OPPOSITE: This seating area includes one of my absolute favorite chairs, the Egg chair by Arne Jacobsen. It's complemented by a rare Polar Bear sofa by Jean Royère, as well as the low PK61 coffee table by Poul Kjaerholm and the marble-top Biedermeier occasional table. They all sit on top of an antique Malayer rug from the early nineteenth century. In the background, I used an eighteenth-century French architectural element as a podium for an antique African necklace.

PAGES 16 AND 17: A Ping-Pong table by Rirkrit Tiravanija fills the entryway. A Spanish colonial bench creates a nice contrast with the Serge Mouille chandelier and sconces and nineteenth-century Agra carpet.

PAGES 18 AND 19: In the main living room, a pair of slipcovered sofas creates a nice seating area alongside a cocktail table by The Melrose Project, Louis XVI Bergeres, the Avalon blanket by Hermès, and a vintage fringed throw found at Pat McGann. A mixed media sculpture by Catherine Willis hangs over the fireplace.

OPPOSITE: This great vintage library ladder displays a mask from my collection of African art. The stool is by Clarke & Reilly, and the eighteenth-century table from Axel Vervoordt is positioned below a vintage lamp from Jean Prouvé. ABOVE: I like creating little vignettes wherever I can, like this eighteenth-century carved stone bust, eighteenth-century Italian table with bluestone top, and a section of a nineteenth-century artist's model.

RIGHT: We added a screened porch for some outdoor seating and paired this nineteenth-century trestle table with wicker armchairs.

PAGES 24 AND 25: In our breakfast room, an eighteenth-century French worktable is paired with a set of stackable chairs by Gijs Bakker. The drawing to the left is by Bill Traylor and the torchiere is by Waldo Fernandez. The cocktail table is nineteenth-century Belgian and sits on an antique Kerman rug from J. Iloulian.

This house had lots of bedrooms because those are important, after all. But we also had a game room where we could play our absolute favorite game, poker. There was a fantastic gym and a whole separate studio where Portia could paint. It was a great place for big parties. I remember one party in particular where I caught Diane Keaton—who also loves interior design— measuring my kitchen by stretching her arms out across each wall. At least I think that's what she was doing. Maybe she was just hugging my oven. Either way, she was a fan of this house and we were, too.

The main stumbling block of this house was the very large living room—I could never get that room quite right, to the point where it felt intimate and comfortable. We worked with Tommy and Kathleen Clements. We worked with Cliff Fong. We adjusted and readjusted and moved everything around. And then we did it again. That's the fun of it for me. When you leave furniture in one place for too long, it gets stale. I have been known to stay up quite late (sometimes as late as eleven!) rearranging furniture until I'm completely satisfied. It's very fun to do. The only problem is when you wake up in the middle of the night to get some water and you forget you moved the credenza right in the middle of your normal walking path. And then *Bam!* You've stubbed your entire lower body and spewed words you only hear in Martin Scorsese movies.

But I digress. We really loved this house and tried to make it work. Outside, we added a pond. We planted a mini orchard of trees. We Garden of Edened out. Then we learned that unlike the Garden of Eden, those trees didn't tend themselves; a compound requires a whole lot of gardening, and a big house requires a whole lot of dusting. In the end we decided we didn't want to live that way. And so we decided to move and, this time, to downsize.

OPPOSITE: One of my favorite features of the kitchen was this custom-made glass display cabinet. The range is by Wolf. The rugs are antique Khotans and Malayers and the beautiful floor is made from reclaimed teak beams from China.

NEW HEELS in 3 minutes

OPPOSITE: We like shoes. This is our shoe closet, with a vintage Louis Vuitton jewelry case and vintage American sign. ABOVE: The limestone countertops, stained walnut vanities, and Moroccan mirror created a warm and organic feeling in the master bath. The wooden bowl and the low-back Windsor chair are both nineteenth-century American and the seed sculpture is by Kevin Inkawhich.

RIGHT: The antique Asante stool is perfect for resting towels outside the shower and bath. The tub is constructed from marble slabs. To the right is an antique throne/chair from Central Africa.

PAGES 32 AND 33: Here's a view of the exterior of our home with the koi pond in the foreground. We added this after purchasing the adjacent property.

In the living room of the guesthouse, we created a cozy, eclectic space with an easy chair and ottoman by Mogens Koch, a folding campaign chair by Mogens Koch, an antique leather chesterfield and a deconstructed nineteenth-century tufted English chair. An industrial worktable is used as a console underneath the television and an early American cobbler's table sits in front of the sofa. The collection of vintage and antique portraits, including one of a seventeenth-century courtesan, adds some additional quirks to the room. The library ladder is early nineteenth century.

OPPOSITE: Some books and a few trophies on display in and around our nineteenth-century cabinet and desk.
ABOVE: This vintage industrial cabinet was paired with a cozy Victorian settee. The eighteenth-century Italian santo figure, antique medicine balls, and nineteenth-century bronze table added a little more character to the room.

WHAT THIS HOUSE TAUGHT ME

1. In getting started, it's worth considering how you want a room to feel. Should it be formal, casual, fun and friendly, minimal and quiet, warm and cozy? Having an idea ahead of time can really help you in putting it all together.

2. I usually start with a key piece in each room and design around it. In a dining room, it's the table. In the living room, it's the sofa. It's much easier to do this than to add the large, dominant piece of furniture at the end and hope that it works with everything around it.

3. If you have an oddly shaped room, dividing it with different kinds of furniture can help ensure you use the space well. In a living room, for instance, take the largest, most obvious area for seating. Don't try to cram too much in. If you don't have room for a sectional, use a sofa, and if you don't have room for a sofa, use a loveseat. Build around the furniture you have space for. Then use the remaining space as you see fit. Maybe add an area for reading with a nice comfy chair, or a game table for poker or puzzles.

4. If you have animals, probably stay away from owning a rocking chair.

5. If you have the freedom to build, adding a screened porch is a nice way to enjoy the outdoors and feel protected from pests.

6. Books really help warm up any room, even if you don't have bookshelves.

7. Emmys really warm up a room as well.

OPPOSITE: In the guest room, a collection of antique and vintage paintings and works on paper give the room a warm feeling. The Cité side chair by Jean Prouvé was a birthday gift from Portia. The Gustavian dresser, early American basket, and early twentieth-century dress form all are quite handy. But it is the antique Kerman rug and custom-made bed with oak trim that anchor the room. The throw is from Hermès.

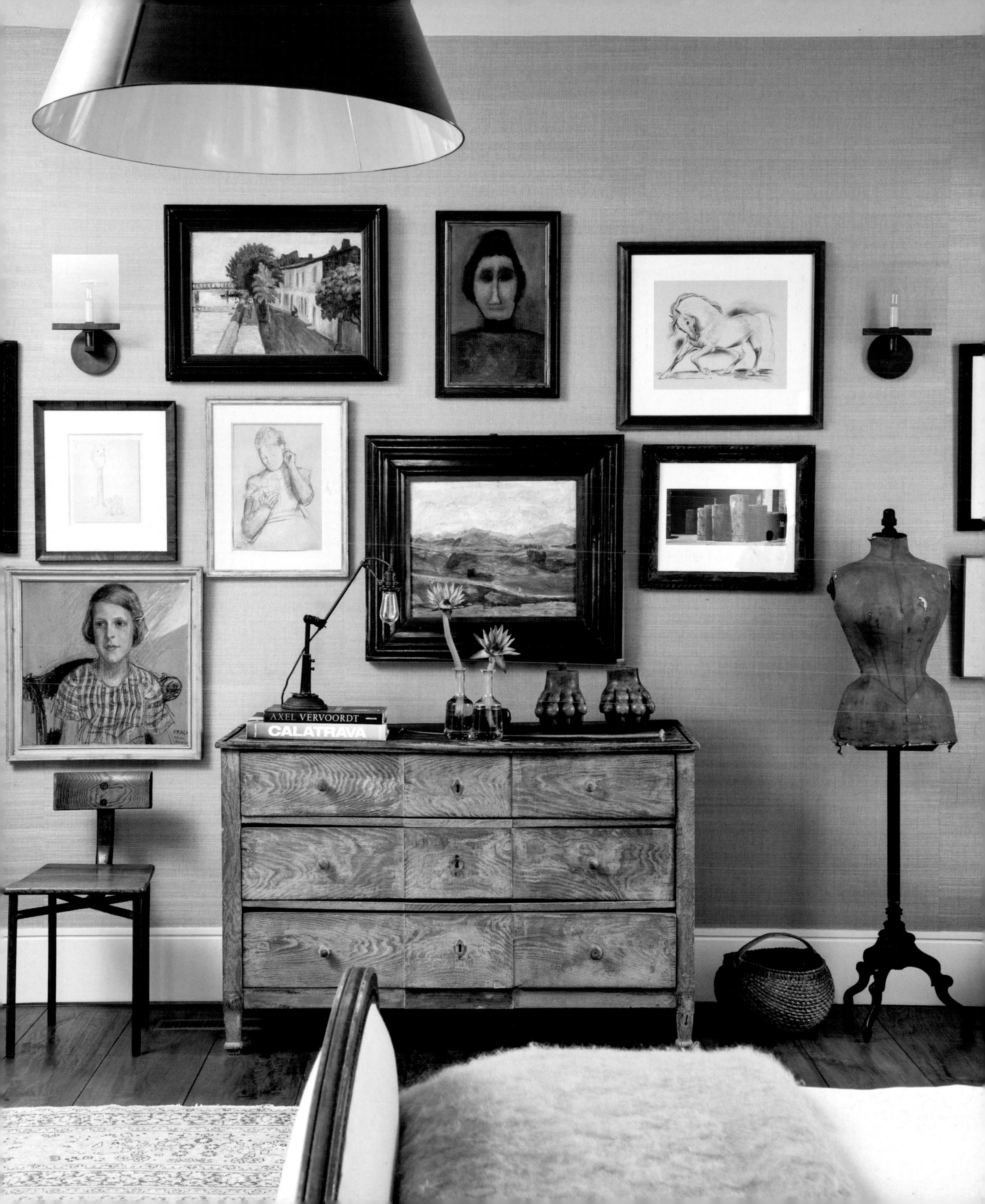
AXEL VERVOORDT
CALATRAVA

HORSE RANCH

Portia and I bought a 26-acre horse ranch just north of Los Angeles. Why? Why not?! It had a pretty incredible past. It was built by William Powell in the '20s as an estate—it then became a monastery, then a rehab center, and then the horses moved in (much to Portia's delight). It was an incredible piece of property, with eight individual cabins, several barns, and of course, horse stables. There were also these magnificent, giant boulders scattered about. The whole place looked like it belonged on another planet.

When we got it, the property had been a little neglected. It was a professional horse facility (I think parts of the movie *Seabiscuit* were filmed there), and the outbuildings that were occupied were really just basic offices. The boulders didn't need to be touched—which is good because, well, they were boulders. But the rest of it needed a revamp, to put it lightly. Everyone thought it would take me (many) years to get it in shape, but it actually took me twelve short months. Want me to decorate your house? I'm pretty efficient. (We'll talk about my fee at another time.) The first thing to go were these signs that were all over the property: "Don't even think about parking there." Wouldn't dream of it. And then I moved on to the cabins and the barns. I approached it like I was designing and decorating ten different homes, giving every cabin and space its own unique identity—had I not, I think it would have started to feel a bit like a hotel. But that was a unique challenge, too, because while I wasn't fixated on making a whole "house" that hangs together as one, I also wanted it all to feel like home. The only real theme that stuck was comfort. We lived in every cabin, as we decorated and restored them one by one. When we finished one, we'd move in and begin work on the next. The first cabin we lived in didn't have a

OPPOSITE: Here we are in the grove surrounding our 60-acre horse property.

PAGE 42: A nineteenth-century Belgian console with hurricane lamps from Lucca Antiques and a vintage American wicker seating group created a nice outdoor living room. PAGE 43: In the Romantic Barn, which we used as a game room, a midcentury American industrial worktable with stone bust of a man (French, 1900s) sets the mood. The leather chesterfield (American 1940s) and a pair of deconstructed nineteenth-century French chairs surround a French turn-of-the-century artist's stand we used as a coffee table. A nineteenth-century portrait of a gentleman and a Prouvé jib lamp above the sofa created a nice lounge area for us.

kitchen, a bathtub, or any other amenities to speak of. But it was fun. Number 8 was the biggest cabin. For no particular reason, we spent most of our nights in Number 5, which had a screened porch and a view of an epic rock (it really was epic).

Eventually, I redid the Art Barn, which we used as a dining room for bigger parties. There was the Romantic Barn, where Portia and I celebrated our first wedding anniversary (I surprised her with some factory lights from the early 1900s that she had seen and loved), hence the name. The last thing I tackled was Portia's Barn, which I learned should not be decorated at all. Barns are dirty. Nobody wants to dust sixteen ornately framed paintings every week. But there were so many cool sculptures and art pieces that I loved in those barns and cabins; I've since moved a lot of them to other houses and even to my office and dressing room at work. My staff isn't allowed to touch anything, but they are free to admire from afar.

While we lived on the ranch, we tried to make use of the entire property so we could enjoy the outdoors. We put in a tennis court and put up a badminton net. It was really fun, especially when I won. And if we didn't have guests over we could always play doubles with the coyotes and skunks that roamed the property. They were a joy. That is one thing I really loved about the ranch—we were so close to Los Angeles but able to feel secluded in a natural wonderland. Portia and I would bring out big picnic blankets and just lay around, surrounded by wild flowers and huge oak trees. When we were there instead of in the city, this really felt like our home away from home. I have to say, the ranch has been one of my favorite projects to date.

PAGES 44 AND 45, LEFT: In one alcove of the barn I placed a large early twentieth-century American worktable, vintage wicker chair, and French early nineteenth-century deconstructed bucket chair to have a nice place to sit. I hung the twentieth-century ornithology prints myself one afternoon. CENTER: A French nineteenth-century Os de Mouton settee (with vintage suzani textile pillows) sits against a backdrop of early twentieth-century German equestrian heritage duffles. Opposite the seating area an early twentieth-century Belgian worktable is used as a console, and holds a nineteenth-century African mask and assorted vintage Italian terra-cotta pots. RIGHT: A horse.

OPPOSITE: We reused our stacking chairs by Gijs Bakker around a nineteenth-century oval table in the kitchen of our main cabin. There's an unusual nineteenth-century Swedish rug below. The chandelier is early twentieth-century by O. C. White. In the background, you can see the painted wood cabinetry and bluestone countertop as well as part of my collection of early American hand-carved bowls and stools, with vintage fencing masks from Europe.

PAGES 48 AND 49: This was the first fully realized cabin. I mix and matched a set of early American Windsor chairs around a nineteenth-century stone-top table from Belgium. The kitchen has a custom bluestone counter and sink with stained oak cabinet. A vintage industrial shelving unit displays my collection of nineteenth-century African masks, taxonomy drawings, and American primitive artifacts. The vintage Moroccan rug in front of the fireplace feels fresh with Danish midcentury lounge chairs. The chest behind them is Gustavian.

RIGHT: The custom sofa by Brenda Antin, Scimitar chair by Ib Kofod-Larsen, and contemporary bluestone coffee table made for a comfortable living room in this cabin. Books, along with a French artist's model of a horse and a figurine, flank the chipped, stack stone fireplace. The rug is hemp, handwoven in Tibet.

PAGES 52 AND 53: We used this barn like a dining room and kitchen. This seating area is made up of Danish leather armchairs, a bluestone coffee cocktail table, a pair of antique armchairs in Belgian linen, and a vintage leather chesterfield. On the floor is a nineteenth-century tribal carpet, and on the wall hangs an eighteenth-century Spanish wood ring.

ABOVE: Here a vintage industrial kitchen rack with butcher-block top stores a selection of antique ironstone dishes and pitchers. The nineteenth-century bluestone table and a vintage American chalkboard made for the perfect prep area while entertaining.

OPPOSITE: The dining room of the barn consisted of a seventeenth-century Swedish farm table surrounded by Swedish armchairs, circa 1930. The eighteenth-century Spanish desk, nineteenth-century cabinet, and antique American speed bag rounded out the room.

In Portia's painting area, there's a vintage American easel and nineteenth-century French cabinet. In front sits a nineteenth-century French pedestal table with four antique English chairs. The different seating areas, complete with a cobbler's bench and an early twentieth-century American spindle-back bench, made for a fun place to play cards and hang out. A metal street lamp-turned-floor lamp sits next to the vintage American upright piano.

WHAT THIS HOUSE TAUGHT ME

1. If you collect things, rocks, glass artifacts, etc., keep collections grouped in a way that allows for some free space around them. That way the focus is on the collection and not the clutter.

2. Any kind of art can make a great impression when grouped properly on a wall. Framing your kids' art can make a nice statement. An eccentric display can really add personality to your home.

3. Sometimes trimming trees and hedges so you can see the sculptural quality of a plant is better than re-landscaping. Highlighting the beauty nature has to offer can be just a matter of editing.

4. There are many alternative methods to kill traps and poison baits for pests like gophers, etc. Research the best option for you, your family, and your pets before choosing.

5. I love old, used easels. You can use them as art stands or TV stands or leave them to make a statement on their own. And they don't take up a lot of visual space. If you want to impress your friends when they come over, put an amazing piece of art on one, smudge some paint on your face, and make it seem like you've been working on your masterpiece.

6. Chalkboards make a great, fun statement in a home. You can draw on them or use them practically to make lists or write notes. You can write something like, "Remember to put away your shoes," just as a random, not-specific-to-my-life example.

OPPOSITE: Alternate view of page 55.

Next time you're in Los Angeles, take a tour through Trousdale Estates—just one of LA's troves of midcentury architectural treasures. Los Angeles has art and culture in spades—and some of the country's finest architecture.

Trousdale Estates was developed by a chewing gum magnate (true story) in the '50s. So what's interesting architecturally about this house is that it's made entirely out of chewing gum. Kidding! It's not. Mr. Trousdale bought 410 acres in the hills north of Beverly Hills from the Dohenys. (At one point it was the Doheny Ranch, where Ned Doheny and his male secretary were found dead from gunshot wounds…it was apparently quite the scandal.) The hillside was subdivided, and then all sorts of fancy pants people started moving in (Charlie Chaplin, Elvis, Groucho Marx, Dean Martin)—and brought the country's best architects along to construct single-story homes in a delightful abundance of different styles.

I loved living in Trousdale Estates. It had the advantage of being between Beverly Hills and The Valley, where I work, but it was also pretty great to live in a neighborhood where talents like

OPPOSITE: A selection of vintage portraits helps offset more modern designs like the Visiteur chair by Jean Prouvé and a midcentury Italian woven settee. I love old textiles like this nineteenth-century rug. In the BACKGROUND: a large nineteenth-century French library table and another nineteenth-century rug.

An alternate view of the nineteenth-century French library table, with an antique optician's mirror and vintage iron candleholders. An anonymous painting hangs on the wall and a massive wood sculpture by Jean Highstein sits on the floor. **OUTSIDE:** A custom hanging daybed with wool throw pillows by Olszanska.

Wallace Neff, Paul Williams, A. Quincy Jones, Frank Lloyd Wright, and Hal Levitt were given free, single-story rein to design and build homes. It made the twice-daily grind of walking the dogs particularly pleasurable. (Because our dogs are huge fans of midcentury architecture.)

We lived in a Hal Levitt–designed home that was built in 1956 for Charles Skouras Jr., a man who built a whole lot of movie theaters. It is a beautiful midcentury home, one that is full of light and showcases whatever is inside well. The walls were built to showcase art, there were 15-foot floor-to-ceiling windows, and it had an open, marble-lined living room. Before we moved in, it belonged to Kelly Wearstler, who did it up in her signature Hollywood Regency style (which is probably how it ended up as the backdrop to a Steven Meisel ad campaign for Versace). Under our eye, it was a little less glitzy and glamorous. Actually, what I loved about this home was that we were able to make it feel very warm and cozy. We could hang out in the living room and talk and relax. We could watch TV in the TV room and stretch out on the sofa with our dogs. It was just a wonderful homey kind of home. Now that I think about it, why did we ever leave?

OPPOSITE: The library accommodated, well, a lot of books. I love this pair of nineteenth-century French stools next to the nineteenth-century rug. The ovoid coffee table from Charlotte Perriand and the early twentieth-century English chesterfield settee made the perfect place to sit and read every book in the library, which I definitely, definitely did. We used a stack of old wood boxes as a side table.

PAGES 66 AND 67: My gift from Portia, the Cité side chair by Jean Prouvé, shows up in just about every house. Here it is with a nineteenth-century child's bicycle. There are two pairs of lounge chairs here, one pair by architect and designer Oscar Niemeyer, and one pair by Sergio Rodrigues. The custom sofa is by The Melrose Project and the carpenter's coffee table is midcentury.

RIGHT: This eighteenth-century Belgian table also moves with us everywhere we go. On top you'll see an early twentieth-century European bust and early Californian pottery. A French nineteenth-century wingback chair is off to the side.

ABOVE: Here's a detail of a sculpture by J. B. Blunk. **OPPOSITE:** A detail of a sculpture by Ruth Asawa. A custom table lamp by Blackman Cruz is on one side and an antique terra-cotta vase from Burkina Faso and vintage African metal vessels are on the other.

WHAT THIS HOUSE TAUGHT ME

1. Design your home with what inspires you. Use your favorite things as a departure point—whether it's art or architecture, plants, textiles, or fashion—whatever sparks your creativity is a great place to start.

2. Defining the way you live and the look of your home can be as easy as getting dressed in the morning. Just start with the everyday basics and work your way around the room. Add some accessories for accent.

3. I like neutral colors with stronger colors in art, pillows, or a nice throw. Big color statements on walls or furniture can be fun, but limit the possibility of changes.

4. Always think of the optimal view of a room. This could be from where you see it the most, how you enter it, or where the light comes from. For example, in an open floor plan, it's better to not have to look at the back of a tall sofa or chair. Benches or daybeds can offer you nice accent seating without blocking the view of the room. Arrange the room so when you walk into it, it looks open and engaging.

5. Always make sure you maximize a view or make sure a room plays to a natural light source. You wouldn't want to always have your back to a window.

6. Don't be afraid to mix ideas, periods, and price points. Just look for common threads between the pieces you choose, and you can create something fresh and fun. This could be as simple as color or finish. Shape and proportions are also important. A heavy leather sofa might overwhelm a delicate architectural chair.

7. If you spend a lot of time outdoors in the evenings, it's great to have lamps outside. Usually this just takes some rewiring or a new socket and a grounded outlet, or make sure you buy a lamp made for outdoor use. If you're only used to harsh lighting from above, it's great to even the light out with a few different sources. It's also nice to light plants and trees. If it's not possible to do this permanently, there are now battery-powered and chargeable LED lights that you can use to feature your favorite flowers and taller vegetation.

8. Use coasters. Before we go any further and I forget, always use coasters.

PAGES 72 AND 73: The dining table in reclaimed wood was custom made by Lucca Antiques. Leather and teak dining chairs were from Waldo Fernandez, and the unique chandelier is made from a reflective industrial hood. The large nineteenth-century Italian santo was a gift from friends. A nineteenth-century bust of Medusa adds a little more history to the space.

OPPOSITE, TOP: Vintage water bottles. Calendar, American, turn of the century.
OPPOSITE, BOTTOM: A reclaimed wood table and vintage wicker. Vintage American ceramic vessels were turned into lamps and a nineteenth-century candleholder was made from an altarpiece.

PAGES 78 AND 79: The antique stone column makes a nice stand for our sculpture of a kiwi. The eighteenth-century Belgian farm table lines the entry corridor with vintage Oaxacan candle lanterns and a brutalist sculpture of a pig. To the left of the fountain is a sculpture by Harry Kivijärvi, 1973, and to the right of the fountain, early Californian pottery vases.

ABOVE: The early American folk chair from New England, a lamp by Lisa Johansson Pape (Finland, 1960), a nineteenth-century tribal rug, and a vintage American artist's stand with the bust of Medusa make up the entry foyer. **OPPOSITE:** Another view of the foyer includes a nineteenth-century French artist's stand with an African tribal headrest and baroque side table, topped with a midcentury Danish ceramic lamp and an early twentieth-century tole box. The ceiling fixture is by Serge Mouille.

the standard metric system, but the Italian masons and carpenters who built it roughly converted it to their own system as they went along. Crazy. But awesome.)

The surrounding gardens and olive trees are almost as wonderful as the interior. The house truly feels like it was built out of the landscape, rather than plopped on a plot. It feels ancient, like it's been there forever. Like that hill was never without the house. This is a home that honors nature, and I love that. While the house clearly holds Italian furniture and furnishings, I love contrast, and so we moved all our favorites—Prouvé chairs, a Royère sofa, some modern paintings—into these old-world environs. They've struck up a totally different conversation with each other than they did in any of our midcentury modern homes.

If you think of your home as a canvas—regardless of its style of architecture—you can put anything on it. I tend to keep painting the painting until it's so done, there's nothing left to do. That's when I sell the canvas and buy a new one. This is one of those homes that I'll never tire of exploring, though. I've thought a lot about why that is. And I think it's because the house is always surprising. It reveals itself to you in new ways every day. And it's really how I want to live. It's not overly manicured or tidy. It's not overly precious or perfect. And it's a home that manages to be both spacious and cozy at once. I really do hope we live here forever.

OPPOSITE: Just inside the entry gates, I put a collection of antique walking sticks in a vintage lobster trap, next to an early nineteenth-century Belgian console.

PAGES 84 AND 85: Some favorites—a sofa and chair by Jean Royère. The coffee table is by Jean Prouvé. The sheepskin chair by Philip Arctander and the 1960s Danish sheepskin stools are the centerpieces of the living room. The floor lamp by Angelo Lelli provides great reading light, while the Louis Poulsen table lamp gives off a moodier feeling. I have had the antique Guatemalan bench since my early days in Los Angeles. BACKGROUND: The eighteenth-century Belgian table with large Potence lamp by Jean Prouvé above. ON RIGHT: A bench by Charlotte Perriand.

OPPOSITE: The pair of Visiteur chairs by Jean Prouvé and a Charlotte Perriand stool offer accent seating on the other side of the room. A rare slate-top table by Jean Prouvé and the Blackman Cruz table lamp complete the space. **ABOVE:** Here's another detail of the Ruth Asawa sculpture, nineteenth-century stool, and vintage Danish ceramic lamp.

PAGE 88: A close-up of one of the many vignettes in the Villa: nineteenth-century artist's model and antique Italian candlestick. **PAGE 89:** I put this set of Jean Prouvé wood chairs around a large dining table by Rick Owens. The ceiling pendant by Alvar Aalto makes a nice minimal statement with a collection of antique African tribal masks behind it and a handwoven Tibetan hemp carpet below. The floor lamp is by Charles Trevelyan.

ABOVE: In the media room, a custom sofa by Brenda Antin, the contemporary bluestone coffee table, a deconstructed ottoman by Clarke & Reilly, and the antique nineteenth-century American worktable make for cozy TV watching. The ceramic lamp is by Stig Lindberg. **OPPOSITE:** Behind the sofa, a vintage trunk by Louis Vuitton. A pair of vintage wishbone chairs by Hans Wegner and a floor lamp by Blackman Cruz help accent one of the Villa's many libraries.

PAGES 92 AND 93: We spend a lot of time outside sitting around this vintage American worktable we use as a dining table. The wire chairs are from Russell Woodard. The tole lantern above is nineteenth century.

OPPOSITE: In the upper courtyard you'll find a vintage French daybed covered in Belgian linen, alongside vintage Italian terra-cotta planters. ABOVE: A seventeenth-century Swedish cabinet and table lamp by Jacques Adnet.

PAGES 96 AND 97: Here's a view of the kitchen, with stainless-steel cabinetry and appliances and wrapped marble surfaces. Miscellaneous antique Swedish bowls and carving boards are useful for fruit and vegetables. The table lamp is by Blackman Cruz, and dishware by Astier de Villatte. In front of the glass door is a nineteenth-century French pedestal table and a pair of PK9 chairs by Poul Kjaerholm. The lighting fixture is a vintage American industrial piece.

RIGHT: Some additional views of the kitchen, with marble-wrapped stainless steel.

ABOVE: In Portia's office, I put a small sofa by Illum Wikkelsø. Portia's painting tools are in the foreground and a vintage American industrial lamp is in the background. I have to say I love the folk art sculpture of the cat.
OPPOSITE: Here's an alternate view of page 100. A clamp lamp by Serge Mouille is attached to an Aile d'Avion desk by Jean Prouvé. A vintage artist's stand holds an antique African mask next to a collection of riding hats.

Another fun collection of vintage portraits hangs above a bed by Cisco Home. Bedding is by Matteo, with a vintage throw from Hollywood at Home. The room is accessorized with an antique American low-back Windsor chair, antique dartboard from Sweden, midcentury American table lamp, vintage fencing mask, and nineteenth-century workbench.

ABOVE: This antique marble trough was original to the home, but is now used as a bathtub. We use a contemporary stool as a side table. The candlestick is antique Italian. **OPPOSITE:** Back in the courtyard, the vintage seating is by Salterini and the pedestal table is by Jean de Merry. The custom ottomans are by Jane Hallworth, and the custom coffee table is by Cliff Fong. I could sit here all day.

RIGHT: Around the fire pit we have vintage American wicker seating, with a bluestone coffee table on an industrial base. The pillows and throw are in vintage tribal fabrics that add some color to the mix. An antique Belgian workbench offers a little accent seating or a place to rest supplies for an afternoon outdoors. I could sit here all day when I'm not sitting in the other area all day.

PAGES 108 AND 109: I love looking out at this antique Italian column at sunset.

WHAT THIS HOUSE TAUGHT ME

1. I love plants and always plant according to the local climate. I'd never plant a rose garden if I lived in a desert. It's always fun working with local and native plants. If you live in a drier climate, drought-tolerant plants like succulents are available in a huge range of sizes and shapes. The sculptural forms can be amazing, and the flowers even more impressive. You'll get the most out of nature if you plant in harmony with it.

2. Always decorate within the style of a house. You can have accents that act in contrast, but the bulk of what you use will flatter your home better if it's consistent with its style. If you have a stone house, you may need heavier, more substantial furniture. If you have a wood house with old floors, you might want delicate furniture with a softer look. If you have a modern or contemporary structure, architectural furniture might flatter it best.

3. When putting a room together, I like to sit in every chair or stand in every corner and make sure there is something beautiful to look at. And by that I mean a mirror. No! I'm kidding around!

4. Candlelight and scent do wonders for any environment. Burning scented candles or incense in a bowl of sand is a nice way to create a mood.

5. If you're using area rugs, always make sure they are large enough to fill the primary use area of a room. Rugs that are too small can throw off the proportion and disrupt the flow of a space.

6. Every room needs more than one light source. Lighting can be harsh or insufficient if you just rely on ceiling lighting. I like soft, even lighting, and I think floor and table lamps are essential to creating the right mood.

7. I think just about anything can become a flower vase. If you have any old wood vessel, antique vase, metal cylinder, etc., it can be used to hold flowers. If it doesn't hold water, just pick a glass that can fit inside and you'll have something unique and personal in your home to display flowers or branches.

8. If you live in the right climate and you have some good flat land, gravel or decomposed granite is a nice warm and organic way to address a driveway, courtyard, or entry instead of pavement. It's often more reasonable and less toxic as well.

9. Always know what you want before you open the refrigerator door. It's random, but you'll thank me later.

OPPOSITE: Antique Italian column, antique African vessel, and vintage American terra-cotta.

THE BRODY HOUSE

We only lived in the Brody House for a brief period of time. And I don't regret it at all. When you're addicted to architecture and style and design, how do you not buy that house? I was completely in love with it. With its crisp and clean silhouette. With its incredible angles. With its sight lines and nothing except some glass to separate you from the outdoors. It is a stunning home.

The Brodys were philanthropists and art collectors and some of the original benefactors of the Los Angeles County Museum of Art (LACMA), and so it's not surprising that they commissioned A. Quincy Jones and the interior designer William Haines to create a home for them—and their art—in Holmby Hills, a neighborhood that sits northeast from UCLA. In fact, they even convinced Henri Matisse to create a mural for the courtyard (long since donated to LACMA). When the house went up in the early '50s, it was immediately at the center of Los Angeles cultural life: The Brodys were big-time entertainers, and it is a house built for accommodating crowds and showcasing art. While there are a few interior flourishes—a floating staircase, a grand black-and-white floor in the entry—the house primarily revolves around its unobstructed relationship with the outdoors and its clean white planes. It is a "less is more" house: It is a stunning, midcentury masterpiece that

OPPOSITE: In the courtyard of the house we placed this early twentieth-century sculpture of a horse from France. In the background, an original William Haines sofa and lamp.

RIGHT: The entryway, with original hardware on the doors.

PAGES 116 AND 117: All of the courtyard seating is by William Haines. The custom ottomans are by Jane Hallworth and the bronze table with glass top is from Blackman Cruz. The contemporary coffee table with a steel base and quartz top adds a nice organic element.

RIGHT: A stool by Pierre Jeanneret is used as a side table next to a lounge chair and ottoman by Mogens Koch. A pair of easy chairs attributed to Jean Royère are on a nineteenth-century rug.

PAGES 120 AND 121: Here's another view. The seating area to the right includes a pair of metal bucket chairs by Mats Theselius, three vintage PK33 stools by Poul Kjaerholm, a pair of free-form tables by Charlotte Perriand, and the original banquette sofa by William Haines. The custom zodiac ceiling fixture is by Jane Hallworth. In the **BACKGROUND**, a low game table by Pierre Cambrol.

is both sweeping and understated. Sounds impossible I know, but this house managed to both find and straddle that line. It is a dream house, a once-in-a-lifetime house.

It is perfect. But as we all know so well, perfection can be a double-edged sword, because perfection isn't always that accommodating. The home had a rigor, a restraint, and a meticulousness that was really difficult to maintain: It is a house that conceals nothing. It is a house of terrazzo and glass where you see everything—every speck of dust, every tumbleweed of pet hair, every smudged wall, every bit of hedge or lawn that might be growing in a bit haphazardly (i.e., like a hedge or lawn). And when you have little nieces who come to visit, who have tiny, adorable, filthy fingerprints, it's just not realistic. We felt, a bit, like we were living in a museum. And ultimately it was too much. We wanted to live a little smaller…again!

Decorating the Brody House, and filling it with furniture and art worthy of its walls, was one of the more fun projects we've tackled. We teamed up with Jane Hallworth for the first time, which felt fitting, as it was a bit different than all the other homes we'd ever owned. She pushed me to focus on the negative space—to use just enough, and nothing more.

OPPOSITE: In this area of the living room we have a set of armchairs by Pierre Jeanneret, a PK54 table by Poul Kjaerholm, and a chandelier, original to the home, by William Haines. The carpet is nineteenth century.

The custom cabinet here is by Jane Hallworth and the leather table lamp is by Jacques Adnet. Miscellaneous midcentury Danish ceramics and American folk art sit on the shelves. The dining table is by Rick Owens and the set of wood chairs by Jean Prouvé. The chandelier is by Jean Royère, and the rug is a nineteenth-century Malayer.

ABOVE: Vintage nineteenth-century tribal rugs line the entry hall, with a daybed by Jean Prouvé. **OPPOSITE:** One of my favorite compositions includes this bench by Claude Lalanne and the hanging sculpture by Ruth Asawa.

OPPOSITE, TOP LEFT: A nineteenth-century English library table with a midcentury American bronze sculpture of a horse. The ceiling fixture is by Louis Poulsen. **TOP RIGHT:** An anonymous vintage Danish chair and a folk art sculpture of a wolf's head. **BOTTOM LEFT:** A little grouping of vintage artwork, along with nineteenth-century wood trays and an early twentieth-century European stone bust, helps warm up the stainless-steel kitchen. **BOTTOM RIGHT:** Detail of top left. **BELOW:** The kitchen is comprised of marble and stainless-steel surfaces and stained walnut cabinetry. A collection of vintage items, Danish ceramics, and a seventeenth-century portrait of a courtesan are above.

OPPOSITE: Here's the eighteenth-century table from Axel Vervoordt, again with a nineteenth-century portrait of a Moorish boy, a nineteenth-century Kerman rug, and custom sofas by Jane Hallworth.
BELOW: Alternate view of the portrait of a Moorish boy. A rare ceiling fixture by Oscar Niemeyer hangs above a midcentury carpenter's coffee table, an original Egg chair and ottoman by Arne Jacobsen, and miscellaneous midcentury American sculptures.

PAGES 132 AND 133: In the office, a desk by Pierre Jeanneret with an early twentieth-century German desk lamp. I love how the elements in this room came together to create the feel of a dark and moody library—the nineteenth-century ladder, nineteenth-century French wingback chair, primitive French chest, and vintage midcentury Scandinavian floor lamp. The Directeur chair is by Jean Prouvé and the sconce is by Jean Royère.

RIGHT: In the dining room we have an early twentieth-century industrial cart, a stump side table by Michael Wilson, and a vintage daybed by Mies van der Rohe. The throw is by Urban Zen.

PAGES 136 AND 137: The side table by Dupré-Lafon flanks the Polar Bear sofa by Jean Royère. The floor lamp is by Carlo Mollino and both the coffee table and the pair of Visiteur chairs are by Jean Prouvé. The rug is nineteenth-century.

RIGHT: Another collection of vintage portraits with original built-ins by William Haines and a midcentury Danish armchair are found in this guest bedroom.

BELOW: Near the fireplace we have a midcentury American ceramic lamp and a couple of primitive sculptures. **OPPOSITE:** The bedding here is by Simeona Leona. The upholstered bench is by Marco Zanuso and the daybed is by Charlotte Perriand. The throw is from Urban Zen.

The spa had a minimal approach, with a pair of palm wood chairs, marble slab walls, and terrazzo floors.

WHAT THIS HOUSE TAUGHT ME

1. If you are attempting to design a space more minimally, the pieces you choose have to feel special or important. That doesn't mean they have to be historically important or super expensive. They just need to fill a space with enough presence that they make you feel like you don't need anything else there.

2. Try to design one room at a time rather than one piece at a time. It's really helpful to see all the furniture you'd like to use in the room at once. Sometimes you need to bring in a few things to see the room with context. If you have a good relationship with a furniture store, ask them if they wouldn't mind letting you take some pieces out on loan for a short time so that you can make more informed decisions.

3. When finishing a room, I find it's often useful to take one thing away. I always want to make sure it doesn't look overdone or fussy.

4. It's fun to collect art, even if you think you can't. There's art at every price point and art for every personality or taste. It's also great to support young artists. It doesn't have to be new and original or anything precious. Flea markets offer great opportunities for buying art. Putting a piece of art that you love on a wall can really make a room.

5. Make sure each piece of furniture or art has the appropriate amount of space around it to function well and "breathe" aesthetically. When rooms get cluttered, it's difficult to see what's special about each piece you've chosen.

6. Always leave enough room to move through your home and have some negative, or empty, space as well.

7. When buying vintage, condition is everything. I prefer pieces in original condition with a nice patina. I almost always choose something that's reflective of its age, even if imperfect, as it has personality. If you choose well, this piece in original condition can hold its value, especially if it is a piece of design or something collectable.

8. Oh, and never renovate a new home while you're simultaneously getting ready to host the Oscars. It's too stressful. Please, someone, remind me of that should I ever decide to do it again.

OPPOSITE: An exterior shot, with an anonymous midcentury American sculpture.

slickness (I always love a lamp on a kitchen counter). We chose rough-hewn textiles, heavy, well-loved tables, and anything else that hearkened back to nature. When you're living in a skyscraper, it's important to have things that make you feel a bit more rooted to the earth.

The whole idea of buying the apartments was to have an easy, turnkey existence in the city so we could spend more time in the country. And it seemed like something fun to try. But while there's something to be said for getting up on a high floor (the views!), we missed having our feet on the ground. I need to be able to step out into nature even if it means that I have to take care of it.

OPPOSITE: In this seating area off the kitchen you'll see the PK61 coffee table with slate top by Poul Kjaerholm and a nineteenth-century Italian santo. In the background, a handwoven Tibetan carpet; a stool by Dominique.

RIGHT: The side chair is attributed to Marcel Breuer. The PK33 stool is by Poul Kjaerholm and the table lamp is by Charlotte Perriand. I absolutely love this suspension cabinet by Jean Prouvé.

PAGES 150 AND 151: Again we paired the Rick Owens dining table with the set of wood Standard chairs by Jean Prouvé. The midcentury architectural floor lamp is American, and the deconstructed chair is by Clarke & Reilly. In the living room, we have two sofas for seating. One is custom by The Melrose Project, the other a 1940s English vintage tufted leather. Filling out the room is a Richard Neutra side table with drawers, a nineteenth-century Belgian bench, a large worktable from New England, nineteenth-century Belgian candlestick lamps with tole shades, and an eighteenth-century Italian leather candlestick holder.

Here's a close-up of a Standard chair and Aile d'Avion desk, both by Jean Prouvé

RIGHT: In this seating area we have a sofa by William Haines, coffee table and stools by Charlotte Perriand, leather Swan chair by Arne Jacobsen, magazine stand by Jacques Adnet, and a Mathieu Matégot lounge chair.

PAGES 156 AND 157: This is a great little reading nook. That's a Jean Royère daybed with a pillow in vintage tribal fabrics, the PK61 coffee table with slate top from Poul Kjaerholm, and a vintage African stool. The ceramic dish on the table is by Arne Bang.

I love the simplicity of this bedroom. The custom Jane Hallworth bed is flanked by two nineteenth-century Belgian side tables. A nineteenth-century Swedish chest sits at the foot of the bed. The table lamp is by Jacques Adnet, the sconce by Serge Mouille. Bedding is by Simeona Leona and the ceramic bowl is by Arne Bang.

WHAT THIS HOUSE TAUGHT ME

1. Paint can do wonders for rooms that might need a little personality. Painting a whole room can change it dramatically, but sometimes just painting one wall can really add a nice dynamic to an otherwise basic space.

2. When choosing paint colors, put a few different tones of your favorite color up on a couple of different walls. Make sure you look at them in natural light. Reflective light, window tints, and other finishes can all affect the way we see color. So what looks good on a paper sample might be completely different on a wall in your home. Also, sometimes you need to see a few colors on the wall, even if they might be wrong, to know what's right.

3. Finishes can make or break a space. If you happen to have a space that's slick or cold, softening the look with raw or aged floors can really warm it up. Shiny countertops when honed can be much friendlier as well.

4. Details are really important. Creating an overall look is great, but attention to detail can really make your environment even more special. I like having a box on a table to conceal TV remotes. It's nice to have a basket to the side of a sofa for magazines or throws if it gets chilly, or even for pet toys. If you use bar soap, I like using vintage ceramic dishes over a regular soap dish.

5. Dimmer switches make a big difference in setting the tone or mood of the room. I have them installed in every room. For floor and table lamps, you can find plug-in dimmers with a tabletop pad for light adjustment.

6. You can hoist anything over a balcony if you just believe.

LEFT: In this close-up of the living room are a Belgian candlestick lamp with tole shade and a primitive African mask, both sitting on an early twentieth-century American worktable.

BIRDHOUSE

This house, which was redone by the architecture firm Marmol Radziner, sits up in the hills above Hollywood, and catches a pretty stunning glimpse of downtown LA from most of its rooms. As far as the rooms go in this house, there aren't that many. It's essentially a modern California ranch that doesn't feel overwhelming for two people and a bunch of animals. And I love the fact that everything is centered around the heart of the home: the open kitchen, living room, and dining room.

To make it feel even more connected, the entire home—both inside and outside—uses only a handful of materials. I don't mean you can fit all the materials of my house in one hand. That would be crazy and so tiny! I mean that just a few types of materials are used throughout the whole house. Slabs of stones are used in the rooms, on the walkways, and on the pool deck. The couches outside are crafted from a continuous stream of the same rock. We call them our rocking chairs. Because of the use of the rock. I know they're not technically chairs, they're more like rocking benches or rocking couches, but we just try to keep things light and have some fun. Anyway. Also, all over the inside of the house, there are these beautiful built-ins made out of walnut wood. Everything has a natural feel and continuous flow, which makes me very happy.

OPPOSITE: I do love these three sheep by Claude Lalanne.

PAGES 164 AND 165: The living room includes a sofa and chair in the style of Jean Royère from Waldo Fernandez, a coffee table by Charlotte Perriand, and a bench by Jean Royère. The handwoven Tibetan hemp carpet is from Woven Accents and, again, the suspension cabinet by Jean Prouvé.

In the entry, a pair of stools
by Charlotte Perriand, a vintage
midcentury candelabra, and
African vintage metal vessels
add some character.

ABOVE: Detail of page 169. **OPPOSITE:** The free-form table by Charlotte Perriand can be used as a desk or a dining table. The chairs are Directeur chairs by Jean Prouvé and the chandelier is a 1960s Stilnovo.

One of my favorite features is the fact that there are very few exterior walls. Again, allow me to clarify. The house has walls. But they're mostly made up of huge sliding glass doors, which open seamlessly to the outdoors with no visible break. So at times the house appears to have no walls. You might think that would present some challenges—like walking straight into a sliding glass door when you think it's open but it's not. (My eye! etc.) Or not being able to hang art on the walls. Or having the hot sun beat down on you from every angle on account of the transparent qualities of glass. And you're right. But I like a challenge. And I have to say, the views are so spectacular it's absolutely worth it.

While the house is by no means tiny, it's one of the more manageable homes we've ever lived in. I really think there's something to be said for owning a home you can inhabit fully, a home with rooms you actually need and will use, and nothing more. The energy feels really right here; the home feels full. Who knows, we might just stick around for a while.

OPPOSITE: The vintage Moroccan rug adds a different kind of casual elegance to the bedroom with a PK33 stool by Poul Kjaerholm and a high-back seal chair by Ib Kofod-Larsen.

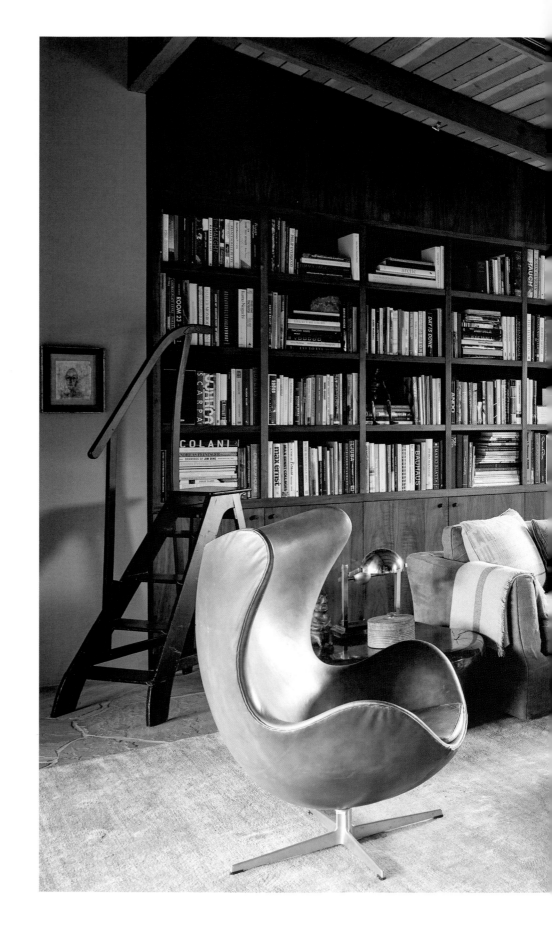

The linen sofa is custom made by The Melrose Project. Pairing it with sculptural forms like Arne Jacobsen's Egg and Swan chairs, and a sheepskin chair by Flemming Lassen make for a nice mixture of forms. The various lighting sources, including the Andrée Putman table lamp, the three-armed Arteluce floor lamp, and the floor lamp by Serge Mouille, add atmosphere. The ebonized stump is from Blackman Cruz and the stump side table is by Michael Wilson. The vintage coffee table is made from an artist's tarp.

PAGES 174 AND 175: In Portia's dressing room, we have a contemporary Moroccan rug, a coffee table by Michael Wilson, Voyage seating by Roche Bobois, and a dresser by George Nakashima. The large sconce is by Jean Royère. The vintage easel is used as a TV stand.

RIGHT: In this bedroom, we have a pair of articulating Italian sconces from the 1950s over the bed, which is draped in vintage linen bedding by Simeona Leona and a bedspread by Hollywood at Home. The large vase is by Gambone. In the background, a Prouvé jib lamp and table lamp by Georges Jouve add some interest to the countertop and **ON RIGHT**, a PK33 stool by Poul Kjaerholm.

PAGES 178 AND 179: In Portia's vanity area, a table and chair by Jean Royère sit on top of a contemporary Moroccan textile rug. An midcentury Italian floor lamp is on one side of the table while a Marc Bankowsky astracan stool with bronze sheep legs is on the other. The mirror is nineteenth-century French. **ON THE TABLETOP:** Midcentury American vanity mirror. **LEFT:** Dress form is early twentieth-century American.

WHAT THIS HOUSE TAUGHT ME

1. Try vintage pottery and ceramics and mix these with new planters for your patio. They really add mood and character.

2. Natural stone floors can give a nice organic feeling to your home and a warmer look than stone tile.

3. Strive for balance in a room. This doesn't mean that things need to be symmetrical; it just means that the collective weight of furniture and objects can't all be on one side of a room. Pieces with height or bulk don't often pair well with short and delicate pieces, so choosing furnishings with good proportional relationships can really make a difference.

4. Vintage fabrics can help personalize your home. They can be used for throw pillows, upholstery on a headboard—even a dog bed.

5. If you buy good furniture, you can take it anywhere. Buying special pieces will always work for you, and a special piece will end up elevating everything in its company.

6. If you have a home with big, glass, floor-to-ceiling windows always know what day your gardeners are coming and dress accordingly.

RIGHT: Bench by Claude Lalanne.

FRIENDS AND COLLABORATORS

RAY AZOULAY

In 2001, Ray Azoulay opened Obsolete (see page 289) in a small sliver of storefront in Venice, California. It has since expanded significantly and relocated to Culver City. Before Obsolete, Ray worked in men's fashion at a major department store, where he oversaw the design and development of dozens of clothing lines and, in turn, thousands of pieces per season. In many ways, Obsolete couldn't be more of a departure. It is, after all, the ultimate palate cleanser. It's the sort of space that, within minutes, can inspire you to overthrow your entire design sensibility, strip your living room bare, and begin again. "I'm always surprised when someone actually buys something," he explains. "I just play in here—I see my responsibility as a curator to motivate and inspire, not so much to sell."

When you enter the store, you are immediately struck by the fact that it feels like another time, another place, and another universe. For one, each room and each vignette is pieced together like it's a movie set. But the mix of furniture, art, and objects is so varied and far-flung that it establishes itself as its own period. In one small corner you'll see a lighting fixture from the '70s hung above a santo from the nineteenth century, on a farm table from the '20s, sitting below a drawing completed last week. "I wanted to create a place where art and objects could exist

OPPOSITE: Ray's one-bedroom loft apartment is a bit like stepping into a white lacquer box. Floor paint can be tough, particularly when you're the owner of an Irish wolfhound named Levi, who is roughly the size of a horse, but Ray solved it by using high-gloss Interlux Brightside yacht paint, which can be wiped clean. Ray is also not precious about floor space, giving wide berth to an oxidized and oversized sculpture. In the back, a drawing by Ethan Murrow, the grandson of the journalist Edward R. Murrow. Ethan's large-scale pencil drawings (yes, pencil) are fantastic.

PAGES 186 AND 187: This is Ray's version of a living room. He would like people to sit, relax, and converse on wooden chairs that are more than one hundred years old. To be fair, the metal and wood one is only about twenty years old, and was designed by Rei Kawakubo of Commes des Garçons, but it still doesn't look super cozy. The one in the back is a George Walton Abingwood elbow chair from England, circa 1897. The life-size drawing model is there to moderate the conversation. The oil painting in the back is by Goran Djurović.

ABOVE: An alternate view of the living room. **OPPOSITE:** A plaster statue of a young boy hangs out next to a pair of cerulean blue English Porter wingback chairs from the early 1800s.

together in one space where there's no obvious context," Ray explains. "That way you have to acknowledge an object for what it is, rather than as a 'decorative' side table from the 1900s that goes with an étagère from the same period. This is about shaking up convention and letting a conversation happen with objects from a vast continuum of time." And those objects do not need to be fancy. "The necessities of the past are now the luxuries of the future," he explains. "Like a fountain pen today—that's a real luxury." Translated to Obsolete, the most utilitarian farm table, beaten up by decades of hard use, looks more like a shrine. "I see the future through the past." That is not to say he can read your fortune if you ask him to, and I realize that now.

One of the things that I've always loved about Ray is that he goes to the ends of the earth to find amazing treasures, but he acknowledges that he's just a small footnote in a piece's larger and longer life. "We might repair the leather in a chair if it's torn," he explains, "but I would never take the imperfections or scratches out of something. The years of wear are the story and the spirit—there is a perceptible soul in these pieces—we are fortunate to just be able to move them along." And the pieces do move. Every time I stop by, the store looks completely different and I think I've walked into the wrong place. Now I will admit that one time I did walk into the wrong place, but that's because I'd just come from a boozy brunch.

Everything Ray has is exquisite and interesting, whether it's an Amanda Demme photograph printed on canvas or a club chair. "I'm going to steal a quote from Thom Mayne here, but 'I am less interested in traditional beauty and more interested in what's compelling,'" he adds. Ray is also not interested in comfort. Don't even think about buying a sofa you intend to actually sit on here, as you'd be better off just sitting on the floor: "Comfort is an accident. Aesthetics and form come first." A motto that's evidenced by his one-bedroom loft apartment, which reads more like an extension of Obsolete than a home. Ray breaks all the rules there, too.

OPPOSITE: His kitchen: Ray ripped out the preexisting Ikea storage, arguing that all his kitchen belongings can fit on a shelf and are compelling enough that he doesn't mind leaving them out.

PAGES 192 AND 193: Ray doesn't care about traditional spatial relationships, as you can see by his absolutely gigantic kitchen worktable and massive chest of primitive drawers. The table, which doubles as an island and dining area, is totally out of traditional scale, but it works, demonstrating, that you can pretty much ignore all the rules.

I love Ray's monk-like, ascetic bedroom—it is humble, and calm, and contains nothing more than what's absolutely necessary. This means a Thonet bentwood mirror from the early 1900s and a sole bedside table. The mirror reflects a piece by Robert and Shana ParkeHarrison.

THOUGHTS, IDEAS, AND ADVICE FROM RAY

1. Authenticity is created over great amounts of time and not out of a can, bottle, or some clever technique.

2. The most important artist/designer is probably "anonymous." Objects don't need an official pedigree to be wonderful.

3. If you're bored, it's because you're boring.

4. Be wary of fridge blindness: When you let your home get stagnant, it can become impossible to actually "see" what's there.

5. Pick your battles: For me, aesthetics and form will always trump comfort. But that's how I want to live.

6. It is very difficult to do minimalism in a home: If the room holds together when you keep taking away, you will know that it works.

7. Don't coordinate: Great design isn't about matching periods and styles, it's about creating a conversation between objects, in an entirely new context.

8. I despise trends and especially trend forecasting.

9. Sometimes the most humble objects—a beaten-up farm table, an old leather chair—are the most beautiful and the most soulful. When you're hunting for treasure, look at what's holding up the mess.

10. The blessing is I see everything; the curse is I see everything.

11. Don't cover up an object's imperfections or story—age often makes everything better. It can be hard to suppress the idea that something is precious, particularly if you paid a lot for it, but use it, touch it, let it be destroyed a bit by everyday life. It deepens its story and adds soulfulness.

12. Never obstruct a view: Make sure that whatever you add to a space keeps the form of what is there.

13. I've been blessed with the gift of certainty…some experience helps, but it begins with good design DNA. It's just a blessing, perhaps better than DNA for long straight blond hair, though sometimes I wish I had the hair.

14. Everyone should mind their own business and pay attention.

15. "Paralysis by analysis" is a hole many people fall into. Too many choices is not good, as they do not serve the end result. They just add noise and confusion. Choose your top three and then go from there. You'll be fine.

16. If you think hiring a professional is expensive, try hiring a non-professional.

17. It is very important to know what you don't know.

18. Lastly…don't run with a stick in your mouth.

OPPOSITE: A day lounge from the eighteenth century, upholstered with the remnants of an old American postman's bag and French feedbag, takes pride of place in the loft's main thoroughfare. Ray doesn't really care about putting furniture in places where people might actually sit (though it's hypothetically a lovely spot); he primarily cares about whether the object looks right in the space.

ADAM BLACKMAN

About twenty years ago, Adam Blackman and David Cruz (see page 214) met at an antique furniture market. At the time Adam had left his job at Abell Auction Company, where he had spent his days buying giant estates (and accumulating an insane amount of knowledge about the history of furniture and art), and had set up his own stall at the market. David also had a stall, and his was filled with furniture and arts and crafts from Mexico that he had sourced on frequent trips home. Adam and David are very different—they're like oil and water or peanut butter and jelly. But that's what makes them a wonderful team. You put them together and you get a delicious salad dressing or a satisfying lunch sandwich. After they met, it made perfect sense for them to ditch the market and open their own permanent store together. It's called Blackman Cruz (see page 303), because Adam's last name is Blackman and David's last name is Cruz. So they put the names together to—you probably figured that out.

Anyway, here's one of the differences between Adam and David: Adam can sniff out a valuable designer name in a 12,000-foot warehouse of junk, while David doesn't care who made it so long as it speaks to his soul. So it isn't a big surprise that Adam's home is filled with things that have a rich history of design. In fact, the house itself has a rich history. Adam and his wife, Kate (who he also coincidentally met at the antique market—what a special place!), live in an A. Quincy Jones home in Crestwood Hills, a neighborhood in Brentwood that features thirty-one of the architect's homes. They were built for middle-income families in the '50s. There were plans to build 500 of them, but plans stalled after only 160 were built, and 60 of those that were constructed burned down in a Bel-Air fire. The rest have been torn down or remodeled so significantly that they're unrecognizable.

When Kate and Adam bought their house, it was a mess, suffering from years of neglect and bad renovations. They teamed up with Rick Cortez of RAC Design Build on a multiphase restoration and seamless addition—in fact, it's impossible to tell where A. Quincy Jones ends and Rick Cortez begins. And the added space was clearly a necessity: While the home is officially a three-bedroom, only one actually contains a bed. The rest are devoted to Adam's amazing finds. So if you ever plan on spending a night in one of his guest rooms, bring an air mattress or you may find yourself sleeping on a handful of solid bronze candlesticks.

OPPOSITE: In this small study off the kitchen, a Mies van der Rohe Barcelona daybed nestles next to built-in cabinets. While the built-ins are not original to the house, Adam cast drawer pulls after the originals. The piece on the wall is a '60s needlework from a Playboy Club in Chicago.

RIGHT: Adam collects mechanical automatons, or nodders–popular as toys and in amusement parks back in the nineteenth and early twentieth centuries. The collection sits along the top of the main living room's built-in bookshelves. The two sofas are by William Haines and the inlaid travertine coffee table is by Montici. Objects they've collected over the years are mixed in with coffee table books, making the room feel lived in, rather than overly studied. The floor lamp is by Boris Lacroix.

PAGES 202 AND 203: A love for Montici runs deep. Adam has collected the wall plaques over the years. The bronze flower arranging dish is Japanese.

ABOVE: A tiny den off of Adam and Kate Blackman's dining room functions as a cozy reading nook. The vertical wooden louvres were part of the original design of the house, and they're pretty genius: They provide privacy when necessary, but also allow light in from the living room below. Meanwhile, muted pillows soften the room's original cinder-block walls. Both Adam and David collect Pepe Mendoza. One of Pepe's third eye lamps occupies the side table.
OPPOSITE: Above the sink, you'll see Chinese yokes from the 1900s for carrying water, and a statue of Pan. Adam and Kate weave in little objects and moments throughout the home, even in the functional zones like the kitchen and bathrooms.

There were only twenty leather Seagull chairs made–designed by Gösta Berg and Stenerik Eriksson for Fritz Hansen in 1968–which is probably why it gets so much space to hang out by itself with a view of the koi pond. Whenever possible, Adam looks for vintage pieces with original leather, like this one. The gorgeous walnut credenza is early Nakashima: It cost $275 when it was originally made. The rug is from the ´30s.

ABOVE: A Noguchi bowl. **OPPOSITE:** While objects from Blackman Cruz sometimes come home with the guys (and vice versa), there are a few permanent fixtures in the house: Namely, this Dan Johnson dining room table and chairs, which Adam owned long before he and Kate moved into their home in 1998 (only 150 pieces of the Gazelle line were made). In fact, when they designed the dining room with Cortez, they designed it around the table and chairs, and built the console on the left to be in line with the table, so as not to obstruct the couple's view. The chrome-plated brass and Austrian crystal glass light above is the Miracle chandelier by Bakalowits & Söhne.

In the master bedroom, the original, built-in closets remain, though the Blackmans chose other bedroom furniture that lives up and off the floor, creating the illusion of a larger, airier floor plan. The built-in bed is custom-built by Rick Cortez, the bedside tables are Ico Parisi, and the lamps are industrial.

THOUGHTS, IDEAS, AND ADVICE FROM ADAM

1. Collections of even the most mundane items are interesting.

2. Orchids last for months and don't require a green thumb.

3. Don't be afraid to leave a shelf or a wall bare—try to practice void over volume.

4. Avoid matchy-matchy. It's boring.

5. Welcome the patina that comes with age.

6. Bring in new things. Let things go.

7. Every room deserves a little whimsy.

8. Ahhhhh, the simple joys of goldfish.

9. Treat yourself to the best-quality towels and bed linens you can. After all, you use them every day.

10. Always keep a bottle of bubbly chilled.

RIGHT: As mentioned, Adam is a collector: Objects from every conceivable region and era are set in conversation in the credenza.

DAVID CRUZ

David Cruz and Adam Blackman (see page 198) have co-owned Blackman Cruz (see page 303) for more than two decades. It's a soaring space where their wildly different tastes come together fabulously. While Adam has never met an important piece of design that he didn't need to own, David will buy anything as long as it's good—or as he says, "good ugly…sometimes I buy things that are confrontational, that are interesting." He finds a lot of his good uglies, along with incredible antique crafts and textiles, in his home country of Mexico, where he goes on frequent buying trips. Because of how different David and Adam are, their store is a wonderland of treasures. I've found everything from a seventeenth-century bridge keystone that's carved with the face of a river god to a Paul Dupré-Lafon oak and leather telephone stand. One of them has been featured prominently in several of my nightmares.

What they manage to find from around the world is truly incredible, but it's the pieces from their own label that really make them stand apart from other designers: a walnut stool in the shape of what looks like a molar, a cast bronze chair with a base that's made up of two snakes, a side table that mimics a tower of records. Their pieces are funny, luxurious, and undeniably good. They mix in perfectly with other pieces from every era, and sometimes even steal the show. Every time I stop by to see what they've found, I find a different scene. "As soon as we get tired of something, it's done," explains Adam.

It's no surprise that many treasures find their way into their own homes—some that are just irresistible, and then others that linger too long on the selling floor. "I take them home so that they're not humiliated," explains David. "Sometimes it takes a while for those 'good ugly' pieces that I love to find their rightful owner." Isn't that sweet? Every credenza should know what it feels like to be loved. Whatever it is, everything looks right at home in David's exotic Paul Laszlo home from the '30s, which he shares with his longtime partner, theater director Richard Hochberg. Nestled in the Hollywood Hills, it offers sweeping views of Los Angeles. It is quietly stunning, and designed in neutrals and soft colors: "I grew up in the desert of Mexico, and so I've always gravitated to warmer hues. The light in LA is very harsh, too—we don't need a lot of color." I don't think you need much of anything once you have a fair amount of good ugly things.

OPPOSITE: A curtained and canopied outdoor dining area at the home Cruz shares with his longtime partner, theater director Richard Hochberg, capitalizes on the primary reason some people live in Los Angeles: dining al fresco, all year round.

RIGHT: Cruz "likes a little neglect." He also likes a consistent, neutral color scheme, and to layer objects, a practice that unifies objects and pieces that span both centuries and the globe. Along the rough-hewn console in the back of the dining room, a Roman sundial sits in front of a glass radar screen. The dining room table and chairs are part of the Blackman Cruz collection, and the objects on the table have been collected over the years. For the most part, Cruz doesn't prize pedigree above all things: "I like good shape, good finish," he explains. Case in point, he thinks the lighting fixture above the table is from some sort of public space. "A hotel? It's Italian, thirties…"

PAGE 218: A collection of objects from David's travels, which take him to every far-flung corner of the globe. **PAGE 219:** The bronze lamps on the console are by Dominique Heidinger.

ABOVE: One of the more handsome bathrooms in Hollywood. **OPPOSITE:** A parchment and metal Carlo Bugatti throne chair from the early 1900s reigns at the foot of Cruz's bed (he claims that he actually does use it while putting on his shoes in the morning). Heavy drapes, hung from the ceiling, make the whole bedroom feel even more stately and enclosed.

THOUGHTS, IDEAS, AND ADVICE FROM DAVID

1. I really believe in "good ugly": There are many things that I buy that I really like, that are really ugly. They're confrontational, they're interesting, they're often surprising.

2. I am fascinated by place, by patina, by craft. Those are the most important qualities.

3. When you are buying, you have to get on the carousel—there is an incredible amount of choice, but at the end of the day, I always find that there's a story, a statement, a thread, regardless of what I might have started the day thinking I wanted to buy. Keep an open mind.

4. When I buy, I always miss one or two pieces—it used to bother me the whole trip, but now I've learned to abandon myself to the process, not to rationalize so much in the moment or worry about whether it will translate back home. It will.

5. I don't really care about pedigree—Adam is a more tenacious collector, which is a good balance—though I have learned that everyone wants designer objects. I just care that something has a good shape, a good finish.

6. I like a little neglect: Nothing is precious.

7. Sometimes things are just done—they become so mainstream they're clichéd. Before that moment comes, it's time to move on.

LEFT: The entire home is tinged with subtle exoticism. It makes sense, since Cruz spends a lot of time on the road, from Parma to Mexico City, hunting for treasures. In the study upstairs (the house is in the hills, so you enter on the upper level), the walls are lined with bamboo shoji screens from the early twentieth century. They're a stunningly understated backdrop to his grand mahogany and parchment desk by Arturo Pani.

WALDO FERNANDEZ & TOMMY CLEMENTS

Kathleen and Tommy Clements are the mother and son partners in one of my favorite design firms, Clements Design. Obviously I didn't introduce them to each other, as one birthed the other. But if they weren't mother and son and I knew them separately, I definitely would have encouraged them to meet one day, as they both have impeccable taste. Two people I did introduce to each other are Tommy and his boyfriend, Waldo Fernandez, another designer I've collaborated with over the years. And for that I am very pleased.

I first met Tommy and Kathleen through The Melrose Project, a now (sadly) shuttered gallery-meets-store in Hollywood. It was a collective for different designers and vendors from all over the world, and it was filled with valuable antiques and unsung, hard-loved treasures. In other words, everything I am immediately drawn to. It was actually pretty crazy, because as I was driving past the Design Center in Los Angeles one day (as I am wont to do) I passed a new, not-yet-open store. I pulled over to peek inside and made them let me in. Well, I didn't make them. I asked them. Persuasively, using my big blue eyes and pouty lips. But what's even crazier is that I had just read a story in *Elle Décor* about a home Kathleen and Tommy had designed in New Orleans and recognized Tommy from their portrait. Sometimes things are just meant to be.

OPPOSITE: Tommy Clements and Waldo Fernandez live in a '60s home that Fernandez bought and revamped (he added a whole second story, for one), deftly mixing new finds and old treasures throughout. It's pristine: Legend has it that every door is lacquered to high gloss with precisely seventeen coats of paint.

RIGHT: Fernandez's art collection could fill a large museum: Case in point, upon entering, you're met by an Yves Klein *Blue Venus* sculpture, which sits on an Eileen Gray console. Straight ahead, a Claude Lalanne crocodile bench sits below a Yayoi Kusama painting.

PAGES 228 TO 230: A soaring Calacatta marble hearth sets the tone for the blond living room. A rosewood chiffonier by Émile-Jacques Ruhlmann sits in the corner on the right, while an Aaron Curry sculpture towers on the left. The hearth is dotted with treasures: two bronze cat sculptures by Diego Giacometti along with Roman marble fragments.

WALDO FERNANDEZ & TOMMY CLEMENTS

ABOVE: A flock of François-Xavier Lalanne sheep hover near the piano, which fronts a Sterling Ruby painting. **OPPOSITE:** Meanwhile, two eighteenth-century French fauteuils, upholstered in a Gianluca Berardi fabric, create a mini reading nook beneath the stairs.

OPPOSITE: Waldo's living room revolves around shades of gray, though different materials add texture: the bust in the background is second century Roman and the piece above the chest of drawers is Mel Bochner.
BELOW: In the dining room, mohair-covered Ruhlmann chairs hover around an André Sornay table from the '30s. The pendant is Albert Cheuret, the bust is second-century Roman, and the white wall sculpture is by Thomas Houseago. The sideboard is Eugène Printz and the white-and-red sculpture is Lauren Booth.

I met Waldo Fernandez years earlier at my home in the Trousdale Estates, where I enlisted him to construct one of his beautiful gates. Born in Havana, Waldo got his start as a set decorator on films like *Doctor Doolittle* and *Planet of the Apes* (the original, for all you youngsters out there), and I was first drawn to him because he brings a certain theatricality to all the spaces he works with. His rooms are never flat and linear. They are instant worlds that can spring up overnight from literally nothing, yet immediately feel like they've been lived in for years. One of the qualities that I admire most is the vision and tenacity to make a room into exactly what you want—simply because you have the confidence to know that it can be done.

The Clementses are similar, in that they seem to believe any home should be a complete reflection of the person who lives there. While I would imagine that it is sometimes difficult to tap into this vein, particularly if you're working with clients who don't know exactly what they like or how they want to live, they've always been particularly good at channeling me. I think it has to do a lot with the fact that we like the same things—Royère sofas, Prouvé chairs, great art. As evidenced by the philosophy of The Melrose Project—which was about bringing together great objects from near and far—they are unrelenting collectors, too, who never rest until they find the very best things.

Tommy and Waldo live together in Waldo's two-level midcentury home, which is perched up in the hills of Beverly Hills. While he likes to joke that its architecture is unpedigreed, the interior is actually no joke at all: Waldo collects art like the average person collects loose change. There are Cy Twomblys, Tauba Auerbachs, and Richard Misrachs, along with Diego Giacometti sculptures and François-Xavier Lalanne sheep (I have some of those, too). It may be a priceless collection, but thanks to Waldo's layered approach, it feels textured and warm rather than intimidating and cold. He is a man who loves beautiful things—and to that, I can completely relate.

OPPOSITE: The stools are midcentury, re-covered in leather.

PAGE 236: Waldo's bright and airy study: A quiet place to work that doubles as a guest room for lucky visitors.
PAGE 237: Waldo owns so much art he doesn't even bother hanging it on the walls anymore.

THOUGHTS, IDEAS, AND ADVICE FROM WALDO

1. Proportion and scale are key to any design—they help to create different spaces within a room.

2. It is important to play with color combinations and mix pieces both old and new to design a cohesive and thoughtful space.

3. Be cautious of current trends. Think twice! This year's look may not be "in" in the future.

4. A first purchase should be a great sofa or focal point in a room, something that you can keep for generations.

5. All light switches in kitchens and baths should have dimmers—it's integral!

6. When it comes to budgeting, it's okay to purchase less as long as the pieces are thoughtful and functional.

7. Always be prepared with option B...or C.

8. Respect yourself and your instincts. If the architect, landscaper, etc., isn't working for you, cut your losses and go to the source—it's always easier than the middleman.

FROM TOMMY

1. I am very influenced by fashion...like a great collection, a home should have an incredible narrative.

2. There is something to be admired in rigorous tradition as well as in unconstrained impulsiveness. When balanced in the right setting, the result is perfection.

3. I have a difficult time with people who overanalyze design. Style is instinctual; it comes from the heart.

LEFT: A cozy sitting area is kitchen adjacent, with one of the home's crowning jewels, proving that when it comes to design, Fernandez doesn't mess around. A Jean Royère sofa and cocktail table are set against a large Richard Misrach photograph. The floor lamp is Marc du Plantier.

I first met Cliff Fong at the Hollywood department store Fred Segal, where he worked the floor. He was my favorite sales guy. He was super smart and had great taste, so I asked him to do some personal styling for me for an upcoming stand-up tour. And before we knew it, we weren't just stylist and stylee or salesperson and salespersee, we were friends. Sometimes he would even stay at my house while I was away to watch my cats. On one trip when I knew I was gonna be away for a while, I asked him if he would find me some furniture and rearrange my home a little bit. Without exaggeration I can say it was one of the best things that's ever happened to me in my whole entire life. He bought me my first Prouvé chair, he tweaked my house until it was just perfectly imperfect, and we kicked off a working relationship that's lasted decades.

This is why I like working with Cliff: I primarily work off instinct and gut; he works off that a bit, but he also works off emotion and story. He thinks about everything so deeply that he can sort of make you fall in love with anything. He was a debater in high school, so he's quite persuasive when you actually get him talking. I spent a lot of time in high school debating whether or not I was gonna marry Donny Osmond, so we're different in that way. Cliff's really taught me to think about the big picture—to think about what objects meant forty years ago and what they mean today.

OPPOSITE: Because Cliff "doesn't want it pretty," he gravitates to pieces that are a bit more conceptual and esoteric. Some are huge names—Prouvé, Royère—others are humble flea market finds. Here, a Bruno Mathsson Pernilla lounge chair nestles with an industrial side table from the '20s. The painting is by Jim Lambie.

PAGES 242 AND 243: Cliff lived in this building when he was in college. When he heard it was going condo, he threw his hat in the ring for a one-bedroom and ended up stretching for a stately junior six on the corner. Washed with sunlight, Cliff mixes crisp modernity with warmer organics. An armless sofa from Marco Zanuso faces off against a Jean Prouvé daybed and Pierre Paulin's Oyster chair. The stools are Charlotte Perriand.

LEFT: Cliff's collection of furniture is always evolving, which he chalks up to his ongoing education. "It's that saying, 'If you think you're ripe, you're going to rot; if you think you're green, you're going to grow.'" The Mathieu Matégot sconces that frame the Paul Klee above the hearth probably aren't going anywhere (they're some of the sole pops of color), and neither is the brass chandelier above the table. It's by an unknown designer. "That's one of the first pieces I ever bought," he explains. The dining room table is Knoll, the chairs are Hans Wegner, and the pastel is by John Jakle.

Since meeting Cliff, I haven't owned a home that he hasn't touched. Sometimes he leads the entire effort. Sometimes he'll redo something after it starts to feel a little stale. Sometimes he just comes in at the end, after the very last lightbulb is installed, and tweaks it all ever so slightly— changing the wattage of the lightbulb, shifting the placement of a chair or a painting, adding a trash bin or some other element that makes the space a bit more livable. Cliff really thinks about these things. He thinks about how someone would actually live in a space and move throughout the room. As much as he can go abstract, he's also capable of pondering the tiny details in a way that can make other people's heads hurt. All I know is, I've never had a piece of trash in my hand at home for longer than three seconds.

Cliff is a partner alongside Cameron Smith (see page 264) in Galerie Half (see page 280), a home store in Los Angeles that basically embodies everything I've come to love over the past twenty or thirty years. You'll find Prouvé chairs and primitive benches; you'll find the occasional Royère sofa, or Serge Mouille lighting fixture. Like in my homes, Cliff is charged with the display of the shop so that anyone who walks by would want to move right in. Cameron does most of the buying and sourcing and has one of the best eyes for both pedigreed and anonymous pieces in the business. No—make that two of the best eyes.

Cliff lives in a three-bedroom apartment in Koreatown. In fact, he lives in the same building that he lived in when he was in college. (Worry not—he moved out for a few years in between renting and ultimately buying.) It is a gorgeous space filled with light and Cliff's three big dogs. He has a rotating cast of truly spectacular treasures that I often want to, and sometimes do, buy right out from under him: a Prouvé sideboard, a perfectly worn in Illum Wikkelsø couch, along with some really beautiful art from young up-and-comers. In summation, Cliff really knows what he's doing.

OPPOSITE: A well-loved Børge Møgensen sofa doubles as "the world's most expensive dog bed" for Cliff's three dogs. The black-and-white gallery wall above includes photographs from Mark Segal and Shahid Datawala. Cliff found the coffee table at a flea market.

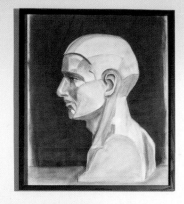

THOUGHTS, IDEAS, AND ADVICE FROM CLIFF

1. Don't be afraid to mix high and low price points. Not everything has to be precious to be important.

2. Splurge on something you really love, especially something with some inherent design value.

3. Buy lots of books, especially on art. Read them.

4. Take a trip to Europe; spend as much time there as possible.

5. Learn another language.

6. Don't be afraid to experiment.

7. Find beauty in imperfection.

8. Experience and appreciate nature.

9. Mix new and old.

10. Live deliberately.

LEFT: Throughout his apartment, Cliff uses antique, primarily Turkish textiles. "I like old textiles," Cliff explains. "Sometimes new rugs look too done."

JANE HALLWORTH

I worked with Jane Hallworth for many years before I even realized that she was an interior designer. I came to know her because I had acquired several pieces of lighting that she had designed, and found several fantastic artists—Kevin Inkawhich, Rachel O'Neill—through her design gallery (see page 295). She would argue that it's a good thing I never knew she designed homes until we collaborated on the Brody House. She thinks that "the universe was protecting her," because her younger self would have been distraught by how I quickly connect—and disconnect—from a home, moving, and then moving again, and then moving again, and then moving again, etc. "Back then, I would have been crestfallen by the changes," she adds. "To find all those beautiful things and then disband them again..." Now she apparently finds the process thrilling—or at least thrilling enough to keep teaming up with me.

We collaborate well because Jane shares my deep fascination and affection for objects that she calls "crusty modernism." While her taste tends to be slightly more gothic (she makes one stunning nineteenth-century-inspired lantern that's studded with otherworldly bronze moths), I share a little bit of her darker sensibility—and a lack of preciousness about the whole thing. I love working with Jane because she isn't about "the plan." She's attracted to certain objects, and then has the confidence to know that they will all come together miraculously to become something

OPPOSITE: Jane's mini ranch in Santa Ynez offers plenty of room for her beloved horses, so the M. Toulouse saddle isn't just for show. It straddles an antique bench that Jane found at Blackman Cruz.

PAGES 252 AND 253: "When the house was on the market, the ceilings, walls, and floors were all wood, and it felt really oppressive," Jane explains. "We used sixty gallons of white paint." That said, she preserved all of the home's wonderful "bric-a-brac moments," like the original rough plaster and the stone-fronted fireplace, which has a little hidden storage space for tucking away firewood. The chair is by Frits Henningsen, the photo was taken in Paris by Jane's sister, Clare Hallworth, and the coffee table is made from an antique chopping block. Jane designed the bronze crow ashtray for Blackman Cruz, and the walnut is Carl Aubock. There's an antique birdhouse above the saddle in the back, and the needlepoint cushion in the foreground is by Daniel Pontius. The other one is Alexander McQueen.

ABOVE: A leather-wrapped Adnet mirror from 1940 is the perfect resting spot for a set of antique rawhide reins. **OPPOSITE:** A view of the corner of the kitchen. Jane designed the square stool in front of the open door for Blackman Cruz.

bigger than the sum of their parts. She told me, "I like to cook based on the ingredients, rather than a recipe." I nodded my head when she said that like I knew what she meant, but I have to be honest—I don't cook, and that really threw me. What I think it means in practice is that she preps as much as she can and then relies on her gut, usually bringing only one option for installs and trusting that it will work out. I like it, because it allows me to create in the moment, too.

Jane learned how to do this not only through her education, but from age, practice, and because she almost lost the contents of her home after an electrical fire a few years ago. "In that moment of panic when I was gathering my animals, and a little token box that had important mementos from my family, I realized that no 'thing' is that important—and that, for the most part, everything is replaceable and people are the most important thing." It left a lasting impression. And I think it's one of the reasons why I'm able to collect—and then part with—so many objects and homes. The world is full of beautiful things and there's always a bit of room for something you love.

Jane's office is a showroom of sorts (and to her, a "design lab") where you can see the pieces she makes and the artists she represents, and get a sense of the darker part of her aesthetic. But the small farmhouse in Santa Ynez that she shares with her extended family is almost the polar opposite. It was built in the '70s by a Danish man who started with a set of plans from *House & Garden* and then went off the rails. He used old, reclaimed wood, salvaged windows from churches, and ended up with a Danish farmhouse where everything is at odds. "I love the thought of having a firm plan and then deviating from it," she explains. There is not a single straight line in the house. For Jane, this is everything: "Because I can't fix it, I can actually relax, enjoy filling it, and love the flaws." This is such a great thing to remember from Jane. Beauty is flawed, and realizing that makes everything that much beautifuler.

OPPOSITE: In the kitchen, Jane uses a mechanic's workbench from Detroit as a buffet and island. In the back, a simple nineteenth-century shop cupboard and a Kevin Inkawich botanical sculpture. The candle cast in the shape of a twig is by Stick Candles. A Nymphenburg bird rests on a Magnolia stump sculpture by Michael Wilson. The cast iron quails are antique Japanese.

RIGHT: Throughout the home, the interiors are airy and spacious, relying more on negative space than a glut of beautiful objects. "I'd rather spend the budget on five wonderful things than forty," Jane explains. The overhead light is Italian, from the '60s. The couch is Ole Wanscher, the chairs are Otto Wretling, and the rug is an antique Persian Kashan. The pillow is Alexander McQueen. A Janine Janet costume sketch hangs above an antique Adirondack bentwood chair on the left.

PAGES 260 AND 261: Jane's trademark "crusty minimalism" at its best: Prized Hans Wegner chairs hug an antique American table, the pomegranate sculpture is by David Weisman, and the Danish crystal chandelier above is from 1900. A 1930s Danish still-life painting converses with an eerily stunning photograph by Ryan Holden Singer. The cherry blossoms are from Jane's garden, and the bird on the console is Nymphenburg.

THOUGHTS, IDEAS, AND ADVICE FROM JANE

1. Fear is the nemesis of good design.

2. Ornament is not a crime.

3. Oscar Wilde said: "Experience is simply the name we give our mistakes." I advocate joyful experience.

4. Mixing eras is like mixing a drink. Don't be heavy-handed with any one ingredient.

5. Listen more and speak less. The pauses between words animate a person.

6. If you doubt yourself, step forward not back.

7. There is no new black. Black is black, which is why it is so comfortingly absolute.

8. Don't hire a designer if you don't want to collaborate. Generally we are not a mute bunch.

LEFT: A simple and understated bedroom. The eighteenth-century blue dresser is Swedish and the Icelandic landscapes are by Húbert Nói Jóhannesson. On the bed, the linens are a mix of Matteo, Hermès, and a hand-embroidered quilt from Afghanistan. The sconce is an early Christian Dell. "The world is small now," Jane says. "I primarily shop from afar and through auctions."

CAMERON SMITH

There's probably no other home store in Los Angeles that captures my taste quite like Galerie Half (see page 280). It is full of amazing surprises. It's where you can find an unassuming and unnamed Swedish credenza, a Jean Prouvé standard chair, a Serge Mouille chandelier, and troves of ancient African beads and bowls, all mixed together. It is co-owned by my longtime interior design collaborator Cliff Fong (see page 240) and Cameron Smith, and pretty much everything they touch is gold.

Cameron does a majority of the buying—he is a crazy genius when it comes to finding great, important pieces for their store. I don't know how he does it. Although I guess I could ask, now that I think about it. After Cameron buys everything, Cliff comes in and moves it all around until it looks perfect. It's arranged in a way that you could lift a display straight out of the store and transport it into your living room and it would all just somehow work. Now, I don't recommend lifting a whole display at once—I tried it a few years ago and I threw my back out. But in theory, it's magical.

Cameron's mother is an interior designer who works in Sante Fe (where he grew up) and Colorado, and he chalks up his love of objects to her—though he claims that she subscribed to the "Alexander Girard school of collecting, where every corner was addressed." They're actually a little like me and my mother. She likes to collect and hold on to things—she moved

OPPOSITE: In Cameron Smith's house, which he shares with his husband, P. J. Faulstick, most of the furniture rests low to the ground. Case in point, this custom lacquered wall unit, made by Flour Powder Pollen. The Acoma vase on the top right is Cameron's most treasured possession. It's a Navajo piece from Sante Fe that belonged to his grandmother. "I had to pry it out of my mother's hands," he explains. The sconces are '60s Stilnova, the rug, circa 1940, is Moroccan, and the large vase next to the black egg is by Carl Harry Stålhane. Pierre Jeanneret made the three-legged teak stool.

RIGHT: The low-slung theme continues into the living room. A four-seater sofa by Illum Wikkelsø faces a suspended fireplace, a Charlotte Perriand stool, and an Axel Vervoordt J9 black slate coffee table. In the back, a Hans Wegner Halyard chair, which is P. J.'s favorite place to read. Like Cliff, Cameron gravitates toward well-worn rugs (and like Cliff, they own three dogs: Jackson, Sloane, and Cissy). This rug is from the Malayer region of Persia.

PAGES 268 AND 269: "I grew up with a ton of stuff—all beautiful and special—but just too much," Cameron explains, intimating why the home is devoid of clutter. A Jean Prouvé Compass desk and pair of Jean Prouvé Standard chairs are the sole occupants of a gorgeously screened-off space, except for the horseback riding ribbons that P. J. has won over the years.

ABOVE: An alternate view of the minimally addressed living room. An Arne Bang bowl sits on the Axel Vervoordt coffee table, while a large bowl from Gunnar Nylund, an antique African figure from the Bongo tribe, and an antique bowl from Belgium rest on the hearth.

OPPOSITE: A Saarinen dining room table from the late '70s with a modified wooden top is surrounded by cane and mahogany chairs from Ole Wanscher. The pendant is by Jo Hammerborg, and the nude is Magnus Creutz (1909-1989).

a harmonica to nine different houses—and I can't stand clutter. Regardless, Cameron is clearly the child of someone who understood how to interact with space. He is a minimalist, as evidenced by the house he shares with his husband, P. J. Faulstick. But it is minimalism with warmth. They live in a cozy, two-bedroom home in Laurel Canyon, perched up high in a grove of trees. Not literally. It's not a tree house. The house is on the ground and there are many beautiful trees surrounding it.

Cameron's style is spare and precise, and he shares my love of a seamless indoor/outdoor space. His furniture is low-slung and simple. Coffee tables and couches literally hug the floor, which make them easy to trip over as you walk to take in the view. (You would think I'd remember that after the first eleven times I tripped, but that's what makes me so lovable.) Tables are unobstructed and clutter-free—even a perfect Jean Prouvé desk in a screened-off room is bare. That is restraint: It's a very meditative and calm way to design.

Cameron has seen everything, and if it doesn't exist, he will make it exist. The rug in his bedroom was pieced together from parts of different Turkish tents. And he commissioned a very talented woodworker named Flour Powder Pollen (yes, that is her real name) to make the low-slung bookcase in his dining room. He then had it lacquered by Clements Design. And he wouldn't be a co-owner of Galerie Half if he didn't own some Prouvé and a Serge Mouille lamp or two. "I don't legally have to own a piece of Prouvé or Mouille just because I'm at Galerie Half," he counters. "But I really needed a desk, and P. J. likes to see in the dark, so the lights were a necessity." It sounds like I wasn't the only one who tripped.

OPPOSITE: While a few pieces of art dot the walls, the room is low-key and serene.

The bedroom rug was pieced together from large Moroccan tents, while a pair of Serge Mouille Antony sconces light the bed. The linens are Matteo, and the chair is an Arne Jacobsen Egg chair from the '60s. I can't say enough good things about linen sheeting: it's iron-proof, and it looks great in rooms like this, which are an exercise in minimalism.

THOUGHTS, IDEAS, AND ADVICE FROM CAMERON

1. When we started Galerie Half, we really wanted to offer pieces in the shop that we'd have in our own homes. We are our customer. Period. That's how I still purchase today: If it's not relatable to my life…then I won't buy it. I never buy anything that is trendy—that's where you can really get it wrong.

2. As a buyer, I try to stay away from re-editions and reproductions whenever possible. We really try to buy honest, original, and pure design that's suffered few repairs and has been well taken care of. That's where the value is. You can't turn around and sell a sofa from a big chain…unless you have a nephew in college who is hard up. In no way am I turning my nose up at re-editions and I've had several, but there's nothing like the real thing.

3. You can desire a piece of design for years, get it, and then wonder what you were thinking. I like instantaneous reactions.

4. Those of you who are thinking about shopping furniture fairs, flea markets, or auctions…just don't. To be honest…I don't need the competition, but if you must, here's some advice: Show up late and bring no cash.

LEFT: The house is tucked away up Laurel Canyon and surrounded by a wonderful canopy of trees. Since their dining room inside is small, they carved out plenty of spaces on their ample deck to entertain. Flour Powder Pollen built the couches in the back, the Safari chairs are Børge Møgensen, and the slatted coffee table is from France.

STORES

GALERIE HALF

galeriehalf.com
6911 Melrose Ave., Los Angeles

While you'd think that the goal at any design store would be to show as many pieces as possible, Galerie Half is a little different. Everything is given plenty of room, so you can actually see what's in front of you—and how it might look in your own living room. Cliff Fong (see page 240) and Cameron Smith (see page 264) also treasure patina and original finishes: Aside from the always freshly painted walls, nothing in Galerie Half is predicated on being perfect. Cameron does the majority of the buying, whether it's PK22 chairs by Poul Kjaerholm for Fritz Hansen, PK61 coffee tables by Poul Kjaerholm for E. Kold Christensen, or antique beads from Africa and primitive bowls from Sweden. Cliff focuses on displays: Everything in the store is placed in such a way that it feels specific and cool, rather than uptight.

LIEF

liefalmont.com
646 W. Almont Dr., West Hollywood

Lief has been around since the late '80s, and since then, it's established itself as one of the best places in the country for Scandinavian design. Owned by two brothers, Stefan and Michael Aarestrup, the 15,000-square-foot space is named for their father, and is a total homage to their mother country. Besides antiques—from baroque to midcentury modern—Stefan and Michael make their own line of Gustavian beds, dining tables, and chairs. They also have a textile line, a gardening line, and a wallpaper collection with Paula Batali. I've had great luck here over the years, finding everything from a baroque stone-top table from the early 1800s to a pair of adjustable midcentury floor lamps done up in brass and leather.

BRENDA ANTIN

7410 Beverly Blvd., Los Angeles

Reigning on Beverly Boulevard for almost thirty years, Brenda Antin is one of the most respected designers in LA—and she's also one of the loveliest. Though Brenda got her start as a studio executive, she and her husband, Michael—a graphic designer—now run their 3,500-square-foot space, where they work on their own line and sell antiques sourced from Europe. It's difficult to go there and not fall in love with their textiles.

BIG DADDY'S ANTIQUES

bdantiques.com
3334 La Cienega Place, Los Angeles
1550 17th St., San Francisco

These sprawling showrooms are a treasure hunter's dream, offering everything from antique magnifying glasses, cloches, and lab equipment to library tables, steamer trunks, and tufted leather chairs. A lot of industry people come here for set dressing, which means that it all has a subtle theatrical vibe. In short: It's not the sort of place where you go for a low-key side chair—everything here has a story, and lots of character.

OBSOLETE

obsoleteinc.com
11270 W. Washington Blvd., Culver City

It's rare to find a store that can so perfectly span so many different aesthetics and feel like it's part of something entirely new, but Obsolete does precisely that. Though Ray Azoulay (see page 184) recently relocated Obsolete to Culver City (it was born and raised in Venice), the new space has lost none of the drama, even though Azoulay swapped dark walls and floors for lacquer-like white. In creating Obsolete, Ray wanted a space that was equal parts shop and gallery, where art can be seen in the context of a livable space, and create a conversation with furniture and objects. Throughout the shop, Ray proves that the perfect balance often lives between two extremes, new and old, precious and found, humble and exquisite. He's also really funny: He's a collector of rare and otherworldly icons, saints, and model forms—many of which are incredibly expensive—but that doesn't stop him from setting them up on leather couches and settees, complete with crossed legs. It's the context that counts, after all. He's always quick to point out that a '70s chandelier might look cheesy in a gallery of pieces from the same era, but when set above a primitive worktable, it looks just right.

JF CHEN

jfchen.com
1000 N. Highland Ave., Los Angeles

The first JF Chen opened almost forty years ago, and they've been adding square footage and opening more outposts ever since. Joel and Margaret are insane collectors—and the extra square footage is very much needed. The first outpost was a modest space on Melrose Avenue—now they have four locations and almost 78,000 square feet of merchandise. I never go to JF Chen unless I have hours to spare, as they've amassed pieces from every era and every part of the world. It was there that I found the perfect Jean Prouvé bench from the '50s, a wire sculpture by Ruth Asawa, and a Frits Henningsen highback leather wingchair. They also have a house-designed line of smaller objects and porcelain.

LUCCA ANTIQUES

luccaantiques.com
744 N. La Cienega Blvd. West Hollywood

There are a lot of things to love about Susan and Stephen Keeney. For one, they named their business after their beloved late golden retriever. For two, they met at an antiques fair: At the time, Stephen was a philosophy professor who happened to also deal in antique silver. Susan, a childhood cancer survivor, had founded a nonprofit and gone on to write and create documentary films. But their commom interests revolved around antiques, and so they opened their first store in Santa Monica in 1999. These days, they have stores in LA, New York, and San Francisco, and a big showroom and workshop near Montecito, where they create their own line of furniture. One of my favorite pieces from Lucca was actually made accidentally. It's a coffee table topped with a piece of black leather that once covered a bench in their workshop. It aged perfectly—despite its proximity to open flames and sharp tools—and they pulled it from the bench to turn it into a piece of furniture. I also found an incredible life-size cement horse at Lucca (actually I saw it before it even made it into the showroom and bought it on site).

HALLWORTH GALLERY

hallworth.us
767 La Cienega Blvd., West Hollywood

Jane Hallworth's office-meets-gallery is "one part showroom, two parts design lab," and a testament to her love of "furnishing small rooms in a really epic way." While her home in Santa Ynez (see page 250) is washed in white paint, she keeps her office dark. "I go in and buckle down," she adds—and burns some frankincense in the process. "It invites good spirits in." Jane designed the stunning Tile Wall (BOTTOM LEFT), and her desk is an Alma Allen walnut table and stumps (BOTTOM RIGHT). Like in her interior design work, Jane's aesthetic revolves around "crusty modernism," which she defines as the right amount of patina, set against the right amount of negative space. And when she can't find exactly what she wants in auctions from around the globe ("the world is small now"), she makes it herself, whether it's in the form of a gigantic constellation light that can be seen at Blackman Cruz (see page 303), or an antique lantern (TOP RIGHT) from Jane's American Gothic line that she covered in cast bronze moths. Everything in her design shop has a price, and it's also a great place to see the work of artists and designers that Jane represents, including Kevin Inkawich.

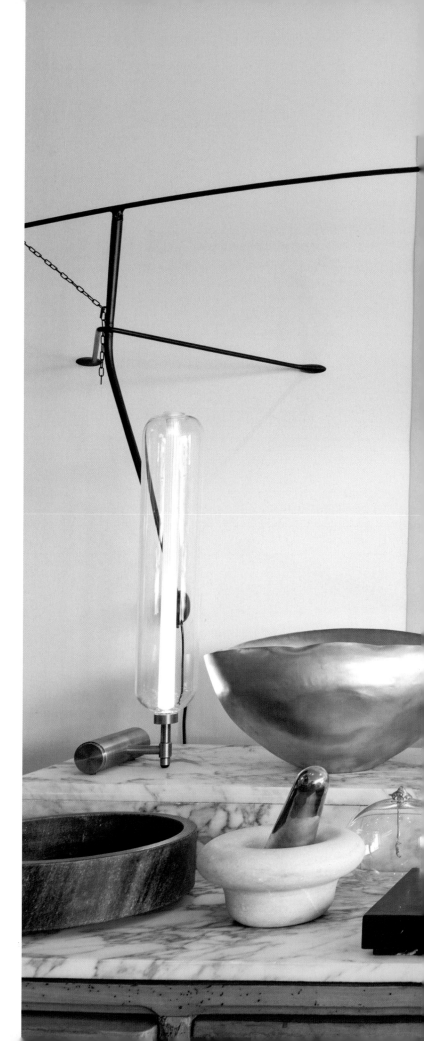

GARDE

gardeshop.com
7418 Beverly Blvd., Los Angeles

While Scotti Sitz's shop has only been
around for a few years, it's so well
conceived that it feels like it's been there
forever. Washed in soft grays and whites,
the emphasis here is on smaller home
accessories—blankets, baskets, dog beds,
candles—from European designers who are
little known in the States, like Michaël
Verheyden and Belgium's Vincent Van
Duysen. There are also some well-known
names like Tom Dixon, Hella Jongerius,
and Lindsey Adelman.

NICKEY KEHOE

nickeykehoe.com
7221 Beverly Blvd., Los Angeles

Interior designers Todd Nickey and Amy Kehoe teamed up in 2004 (Todd had been working as a designer, while Amy was doing hotel interiors for the W), and then opened their own store four years later. It's a great shop. Unintimidating, homey, inviting, and full of both small pleasures and bigger investments. You can find Astier de Villatte plates here, Heather Taylor table napkins, overdyed pillows from the South of France, and Amish rugs from Pennsylvania, all mixed with furniture from a wide range of eras. Some of it comes from names, but much of it has humble origins: I've found a beautiful primitive coffee table there, along with a set of oak and rush chairs.

MICHAEL HASKELL
ANTIQUES

michaelhaskell.com
559 San Ysidro Rd., Montecito

Focusing on Spanish Colonial antiques, Michael Haskell's Montecito shop may be tiny—but it is mighty. Simplicity isn't really the name of the game here, as almost everything is ornate, whether it's a mosaic-laced pair of side tables from nineteenth-century Morocco or a carefully wrought eighteenth-century desk from Italy. Michael got his start as a dealer of Native American antiques, while his son and business partner, Eric, was a commercial actor, and they are both drawn to incredibly unique, often one-of-a-kind objects. I've gotten handwoven baskets, sculptures, and a wild rare New Mexican retablo here.

BLACKMAN CRUZ

blackmancruz.com
836 N. Highland Ave., Los Angeles

Adam Blackman (see page 198) and David Cruz's (see page 214) shop on Highland occupies a giant space that was once the notorious gay nightclub Probe, which even made a cameo in *American Gigolo.* Fortunately, scale is the pair's friend: They transformed the cavernous main room into pure theater. Giant chandeliers dangle from the ceiling, mirrors and sconces inch up the walls, and seating arrangements stretch across the main floor. Adam and David are avid collectors who aren't shy about buying with their guts and showcasing unexpected finds—then, they design and make what doesn't exist. They keep the whole experience cohesive through muted lighting and tight little vignettes and conversational zones, where you can imagine relocating the installation right into your own home. Despite its warehouse-like size, the inventory at Blackman Cruz moves quickly: Every time I step inside, a new world awaits.

ACKNOWLEDGMENTS

This book exists because I have always loved pretty houses and the pretty things that go in them. But through the years there have been many people who have inspired me and taught me about the art of architecture and furniture design, which transformed my interest into a more educated passion. I wish to thank the following people, many of whom I am happy to call my friends.

Stefan & Michael Aarestrup
William Abranowicz
Brenda Antin
Ray Azoulay
Howard Backen
Adam Blackman
Shane Brown
Joel Chen
Kathleen Clements
Tommy Clements
David Cruz
Joanne DeGeneres
Portia de Rossi
Waldo Fernandez

Cliff Fong
Jane Hallworth
Michael Haskell
Susan Keeney
Todd Nickey & Amy Kehoe
Craig Peralta
Lauren Pomerantz
John Saladino
Ryan Schwartzman
Patrick Seguin
Scotti Sitz & John Davidson
Cameron Smith
Axel Vervoodt
Caryn Weingarten

27.
Anton Weis
Killingen
1920.